Jews in the Economic and Political Life of Mediaeval Islam

Jews in the Economic and Political Life of Mediaeval Islam

By

WALTER J. FISCHEL

NEW INTRODUCTION
BY THE AUTHOR

on

THE COURT JEW IN THE ISLAMIC WORLD

KTAV PUBLISHING HOUSE, INC.

NEW YORK

1969

REPRINTED BY PERMISSION OF THE ROYAL ASIATIC SOCIETY
OF GREAT BRITAIN AND IRELAND
LONDON
FIRST PUBLISHED 1937

Library of Congress Catalog Card Number: 68-25719
Manufactured in the United States of America

TO IRENE AND OUR DAUGHTER CORINNE

CONTENTS

INTRODUCTION

THE COURT JEW IN THE ISLAMIC WORLD

1.

When we began, over a generation ago, to turn our attention to the field of the social and economic history of the Jews in the various lands of medieval Islam and combed the then available sources, primarily Arabic and Persian, for relevant data on this topic, the search yielded illuminating insights into the activities of some prominent Jewish officials who had played a role in the economic and political life of their time.

During those years which elapsed since the first appearance of this, our study, new historical texts and sources have become accessible in Arabic, Persian, and Hebrew, along with the research of the Western and Eastern scholars covering our period and region, which provided us with a better understanding of the historical scene within which these Jewish officials moved. In the light of the advance of our knowledge, it is therefore incumbent upon us, for the guidance of the student of Jewish and Islamic economic history, to elucidate again, briefly, the central problems.

The Jewish personalities who are dealt with here were all closely associated with the court or the ruling class and had climbed the ladder of success and influence in the public arena. They confronted us with the phenomenon of the Court Jew in Islamic society, the "Hofjude"—a well-known feature also in the social and economic structure in later Western European history[1]—who by virtue of his abilities and special qualifications, had been called upon to serve the Islamic states and their rulers at various periods in Islamic history in a variety of public assignments and functions.

In order to appraise the full significance of the Court Jew in the medieval Islamic civilization, it has to be stressed that the interreligious attitude of Islam toward the non-Muslims, Jews and Christians alike, living within the realm of Islam was conditioned and regulated by a contract,[2] according to which the Muslim authorities granted "the people of the revealed book" (the *ahl al-Kitāb*)[3] protection and safety, religious and cultural autonomy and free exercise of economic activities against the payment of a poll tax, *jizyā*.[4] This poll tax had to be paid by all the *ahl adh-Dhimma* ("people of protection") in "a state of humiliation" as a tribute and acknowledgment of their submission to the political authority of Islam. This contractual arrangement, laid down in the Koran (Sura 9. 29),[5] expounded in the Hadith and defined in great detail by later Muslim jurists and theologians, established, in principle, a strict demarcation line between the ruling Arab-Muslim aristocracy and the tolerated non-Muslim minorities, between the conqueror and the conquered, the "Believers" and "non-Believers." It deprived the *Dhimmis* of political and social equality and made them basically "second-class citizens"[6] which only conversion to Islam could change.

This legal concept led, in the course of time, to the imposition of various discriminatory restrictions, entailing among others the exclusion of non-Muslims from employment in government and administration,[7] since the *ahl adh-Dhimma,* members of the various non-Muslim groups, were not to be entrusted with any official responsibility which would enable them to exercise authority over the "Believers." The holding of any public office by them was regarded by most Muslim authorities[8] as being incompatible with Muslim law and in complete contradiction to the basic position reserved for the Arab-Muslim ruling class.

The historical reality, as mirrored in the Muslim sources, attests, however, that after the consolidation of the Islamic administration in the newly subjugated territories, this attitude was not always implemented and rigidly adhered to. The very fact that the question of the admittance of non-Muslims to, or elimination from, public offices in the fiscal administration became a never-ceasing issue in the legal and theological Muslim literature throughout the centuries, revealed only too clearly the existing dichotomy between theory and reality.[9]

That the road to governmental service was not blocked to Jews or other non-Muslims became evident in particular under the 'Abbāsid Caliphate in Baghdād from the ninth century on and the Fāṭimid Caliphate in Cairo from the middle of the tenth century. The fundamental transformation of the economic structure in the lands of Islam,[10] the acceleration of trade and commerce on an international scale, the progressive urbanization, the rise of a merchant class, the development of a money and credit economy, and the pressing need for liquid funds for military and other purposes, had prompted many a Muslim ruler, be he a Caliph, a Sultan, or an Emir, to disregard the legal injunctions of the theologians, and to employ Jews and other non-Muslims in the fiscal administration whenever the interests of the affairs of the state made it necessary.

It was this deviation from the basic *Dhimmi* policy which brought about the emergence of Court Jews in ever increasing numbers, and made them familiar figures in the service of the court of many medieval Muslim states.

In making the phenomenon of the Court Jew—a hitherto unexplored aspect of Islamic and Jewish research—the topic of the present study, we limited ourselves deliberately, in scope and time, to three major dynasties of medieval Islam, to the 'Abbāsids, the Fāṭimids and the Il-Khāns, covering the period from the tenth to the thirteenth centuries. Even within this space of time we concentrated on but a select group of Jewish personalities of outstanding caliber who, as Court bankers (*Jahbadh*), as Court merchants, tax collectors, suppliers of loans, providers of rare and precious commodities, mint controllers and treasurers and, last but not least, Viziers and statesmen, made an indelible impression on the economic and political scene of their time.

Thus we unfolded the activities of the Jewish Court bankers Joseph b. Phineas and Aaron b. Amram at the Court of the

'Abbāsid Caliph, al-Muqtadir (908-32) in Baghdād. We dealt with Ya'qūb b. Killis (d. 991), originally a Jew of Baghdād, the architect of the financial administration in Cairo and the first vizier of the Fāṭimid rulers, and also with the Court merchants and officials in Cairo, the Banū Sahl, two brothers from the Persian city of Tustar, called Abū Sa'd Ibrāhīm (d. 1047) and Abū Naṣr Aaron (d. 1048). Lastly, we covered the activities of those two remarkable statesmen under the Il-Khān dynasty in Tabrīz, in the Northwestern province of Persia, Azarbaijān, namely Sa'd ad-Daula (d. 1291), the Jewish vizier under Arghūn Khān and the great historian, vizier, and physician Rashīd ad-Daula (d. 1318), later known as Rashīd ad-Din, from Hamadan who served under Ghāzān Khān and his immediate successors.

Though many more Jews had held prominent positions in the administration of other Muslim dynasties in the East, under the Buwayhids, [11] the Ghaznavids,[12] and the Seljuks,[13] as well as in the countries of Western Islam in post-Fāṭimid Egypt,[14] in North Africa[15] and Muslim Spain,[16] it was in these men that the institution of the Court Jew found its most pronounced manifestation in medieval Islam.

2.

While the new sources did not call for any basic changes in our portrayal of the personalities discussed—except in one instance—they added considerably to the understanding of essential details and shed light, for the 'Abbāsid period, on the institution of the Vizier,[17] on the role of the merchant[18] and banker, the *jahbadh,*[19] and on other basic economic terms and concepts.[20]

For the Fāṭimid period, the activities of the Banū Sahl of Cairo, and their relationship to other Jewish communities in the Islamic East, have been made more lucid through the Judeo-Arabic documents of the Cairo Geniza,[21] which opened many new vistas relevant to the role of the Jews in trade and commerce.

While the new sources pertaining to the Il-Khān period left

our presentation of the activities of Sa'd ad-Daula unaffected, it widened considerably the documentary basis for the clarification of the last of the great Court Jews under the Il-Khāns, Rashīd ad-Daula.[22] The evidence derived from this new material,[23] which included the edition of some parts of his great *Universal History*[24] and additional biographical and historical sources, Arabic and Persian,[25] has completely justified and strengthened our contention that he was born a Jew in 1248 in Hamadan, that he was the son of a Jewish druggist, and that, until his conversion[26] to Islam at the age of 30, he was a member of the famous Jewish community in Hamadan.[27] His Jewish background and heritage is clearly reflected in many facets of his life and work.

The fact that his *History of the Children of Israel*—the first treatment of Jewish history in the Persian language,[28] incorporated into his *Universal History* (*Jāmiat-Tavārīkh*)—abounds in Hebrew words and terms should, in itself, not be surprising, since Muslim historians before him, such as Ṭabarī, Mas'ūdī, Abu'l-Fidā, and the historian Ibn Khaldūn[29] after him, used many Hebrew terms in their presentation of Biblical and post-Biblical history of the Jews. Yet Rashīd ad-Daula's intimate knowledge of so many details in his treatment of the history of Israel, the unusual degree of his acquaintance with Jewish law and lore,[30] his correct spelling, transliteration, and translation of many Hebrew terms, are surely not the usual intellectual resources of a medieval Muslim Persian scholar.[31] All these aspects, together with his continuous association with Jewish physicians and scholars in Tabrīz, and above all his own confession at the trial, have definitely disposed of any doubt as to his Jewish origin.

The tragic end of Sa'd ad-Daula and Rashīd ad-Daula had great consequences for the Jewish diaspora after the middle of the fourteenth century, and no prominent Court Jew is recorded again in the service of the various dynasties in the lands of Eastern Islam.[32] The political and religious foundations of those Muslim dynasties which ruled after the decline of the Il-Khān dynasty excluded *Dhimmis* from occupying any leading role in public life. Under the rule of Tamerlane and the Tīmurīds, Jews could hardly have been invested with any official position. The Safavid dynasty (1501-1732), which introduced Shīʿa Islam into Persia as the state religion, and based its interconfessional attitude on the notion of the ritual uncleanliness of the non-Believers—a view also adopted by the Qājār dynasty (1779-1924)—hardly offered a suitable climate for the ascent of Jews or Christians to positions of influence in the administration of the state and its economy.

It was only in the Ottoman Empire, which became the center of gravity of the Islamic world from the sixteenth century on, that Jews and Christians could once more assert considerable influence on the economic and even political structure in Constantinople, as well as in the major centers of its Asiatic provinces, Irāq, Kurdistan and Syria, as bankers, Court treasurers, mint controllers and tax collectors, thus adding new links to the long chain of Court Jews in the service of Muslim rulers.[33]

3.

It was beyond the scope and purpose of this study to deal with the phenomenon of the Court Jew in the Islamic world in its entirety and in all its ramifications. This challenging and fruitful task has still to be undertaken by students of Jewish and Islamic economic history, and it is to be hoped that this will soon be carried out.

Yet, even before such a comprehensive investigation is available, we can establish, in the light of our present knowledge, certain common features shared by all Court Jews in Islam. Despite the variations of time, place, position and achievement in each individual case, and irrespective of the differences in the religious and political foundations of the various dynasties whom they served, we can discern some common denominators applicable to most, if not all, of them.

First of all, there is the overriding fact that none of the Court Jews, being subjected as non-Muslims to the *Dhimmi* policy, could have entered the public arena at all, had it not been for personal ties with the Muslim ruler or his Viziers.

It was this trust and confidence in them which accorded these borderline figures a privileged position. Among the reasons which must have prompted a ruler to accept their services was evidently the awareness of their ability to open up new avenues of economic wealth for the state, to develop new methods of commercial and banking transactions, and thus to provide the ruler and his Court with urgently needed funds and commodities; and, as proven in some instances, to delay or stem the collapse and dissolution of an absolutist and autocratic regime.

The Muslim authorities must have recognized also that the factor of the solidarity of the Jewish merchant class in general, and their mutual assistance transcending geographical and dynastic boundaries, enabled the Court Jew to perform his official assignments successfully, and sometimes so efficiently that his services were thought to be indispensable. This belief in their indispensability found a typical expression in the case of the Jewish Court bankers of Baghdad when it was stated that they were retained ". . . in order to uphold the dignity of the office of bankers (*jahbadh*) in the eyes of the merchants, so that the merchants might be ready to lend their money. . . . Were a banker (*jahbadh*) to be dismissed and another appointed in his place, with whom the merchants had not yet had any dealings, the business of the Caliph would come to a standstill."[34]

Common to many a Court Jew was also his standing as a pillar of his own Jewish community who, by virtue of his prestige and his connections with the ruling circles, could and did lay his protective hands whenever necessary over his coreligionists through direct intervention with the authorities in their favor.

All too often a common denominator was also the circumstances which brought the career of many of them, at the height of their success, to an abrupt and tragic end. Many a Court Jew had to pay with his life for his prominence, his dedication, and the loyal and faithful performance of his assignments, and suffered a violent death, brought about not necessarily at the hands of his master, but as the result of intrigues, jealousies and greed of dissatisfied Court circles, who opposed the "illegal" admittance of Jews into the ranks of the Muslim administration.

Last but not least, it should be observed that the very existence of such Court Jews in many centers of the Islamic world illustrates clearly the degree of interaction and interrelation between Jewish and Islamic history, and proves that in the economic and political sphere leading Jews, far from living in the shadow of events in their Islamic surroundings, were actively involved in the affairs of their time and were closely interwoven with the larger context of the medieval Islamic society.

University of California,
Berkeley
July 1969

Walter J. Fischel
Professor of Semitic
Languages and Literature

NOTES

1. See Selma Stern: *The Court-Jew, a Contribution to the History of Absolutism in Central Europe,* Philadelphia, 1950; H. Schnee: *Die Hoffinanz und der moderne Staat, Geschichte und System der Hoffaktoren an deutschen Fürstenhöfen im Zeitalter des Absolutismus*, Berlin, 1955, 3 vols.; and Werner Sombart: *The Jews and Modern Capitalism,* New York, 1962.
2. For a comprehensive survey of the legal status of the non-Muslims see Antoine Fattal: *Le Statut Légal des non-Musulmans en Pays d'Islam,* Beirut, 1958.
3. To the category of the "people of the book" belonged not only Jews and Christians but also Sabaeans and Zoroastrians. For an up-to-date survey and bibliography, see the respective articles by Claude Cahen in *Encyclopaedia of Islam,* n.ed.
4. This poll tax levied on the able-bodied males of military age was regarded also in a sense as a commutation for military service from which non-Muslims were free, see *Encyclopaedia of Islam,* n.ed. 1963, Vol. III, pp. 559-562, s.v. "Djizya."
5. This controversial Koranic phrase has been interpreted by Koranic commentators in a variety of ways, as "willing submission," "acknowledgement of this subordination," etc.
6. See Fattal: l.c., p. 367, "Le Dhimmi est par définition un citoyen de second ordre."
7. See A. S. Tritton: *The Caliphs and Their Non-Muslim Subjects,* Oxford, 1930, pp. 18-36, and his article in *Journal of the Royal Asiatic Society,* London 1931, pp. 311-338.
8. The Muslim theologian, al-Māwardī (d. 1058), the author of *Kitāb-ul-Aḥkām as-Sulṭānīya* (ed. M. Enger, Bonn, 1853; Cairo, 1909) would allow the employment of non-Muslims provided they were deprived of any power of authority and decision.
9. Already under the Umayyad Caliphate there arose to prominence Sumair al-Yahūdī (ca. 695) who, as a keeper of the Mint in Damascus, as an expert in coins, purveyor of metals and provider of loans for the Court, served the fiscal administration for many years. See Ibn al-Athīr: Kāmil, Vol. I, p. 492 ff., and Maqrīzī: Kitāb Ighāta al-Umma, Cairo, 1940, p. 53 ff.

10. See W. J. Fischel: "The City in Islam" in *Middle Eastern Affairs,* New York, 1956, pp. 227-232.; Salo W. Baron: *A Social and Religious History of the Jews,* New York, 1957, Vol. IV, under "Economic Transformation," pp. 197-227.; S. D. Goitein: *Jews and Arabs Throughout the Ages,* New York, 1960 and his: *Studies in Islamic History and Institutions,* Leiden, 1966, pp. 219-241.
11. See M. Kabir: *The Buwayhid Dynasty of Baghdad (946-1055),* Calcutta, 1964., Claude Cahen: "Quelques problèmes économiques et fiscaux de l'Irāq Buyide" in *Annales de l'Institut d'Etudes Orientales,* Algiers, 1954, Vol. X, pp. 326 ff.
12. On this dynasty see C. E. Bosworth: *The Ghaznavids, Their Empire in Afghanistan and Eastern Iran (994-1040),* Edinburgh, 1960.

In the time of Sultan Maḥmūd (999-1030) of the Ghaznavid Dynasty, the Jew Isaac, a resident of Ghazna stood in the service of the Sultan and was entrusted with the administration of the Sultan's lead mines in Balkh, in Khorasan.

For further details see W. J. Fischel: "The Jews of Central Asia (Khorasan) in Medieval Hebrew and Islamic Literature," in *Historia Judaica,* New York, 1945, Vol. 47, pp. 30-50.

13. Numerous were the Court-Jews in the service of the Seljuk Sultans; their celebrated Vizier, Nizām al-Mulk (d. 1192) emphatically rejected in his major Persian-written work, "Siāsat Nāmeh," the employment of *Dhimmis* in government service, but at the same time had close associations with Jewish officeholders, tax-farmers, bankers, and money experts who had been called upon to assist him.

For additional details, see also Ibn al-Jauzi: *al-Muntazam fī Ta'rīkh . . .* Haiderabad, 1938, Vols. 8-9 and G. Makdisi: "Autograph Diary of an 11th Century Historian of Baghdād (1068-1069)," in *Bulletin, School of African and Oriental Studies,* London, 1956-1957, Vols. 18 to 19.

14. For the role of Jews in post-Fāṭimid Egypt, in Mamlūk Egypt, see E. Strauss: *Toldoth Ha-Yehudim b-Mizrayim ve-Syria,* Jerusalem, 1951, 2 Vols.
15. See H. Z. Hirschberg: *A History of the Jews in North Africa, from Antiquity to our Time,* translated into English from the original Hebrew. Two Parts: I. From Antiquity to the XVIth century; II. From the Ottoman conquests to the present; with illustrations, drawings and maps, soon to appear.
16. On the Jews in Muslim Spain, see E. Ashtor: *Koroth Ha-*

Yehudim b-Sfarad ha-Muslimit, Jerusalem, 1960, Vol. I., Jerusalem, 1966, Vol. II.

17. For a survey of the institution of the Viziers under the 'Abbāsid Caliphs, including those with whom our Court Jews had a close connection, see the valuable work by D. Sourdel: *Le Vizirat 'Abbāside (749-936),* Institut Français de Damas, Damascus, 1959, 1960, 2 Vols.

18. See A. K. S. Lambton: "The Merchant in Medieval Islam," in *A Locust Leg, Studies in Honor of S. H. Taqizadeh,* London, 1962, pp. 121-130, and her book: *Landlord and Peasant in Persia,* London, 1953.

19. For additional details on "jahbadha" and on "suftaja" see A. A. Dūrī: *Studies on the Economic Life of Mesopotamia in the 10th Century,* Arabic Text, Baghdād, 1948; A. Dietrich: *Arabische Briefe in der Papyrussammlung der Hamburger Staats und Universitäts-Bibliothek,* Hamburg, 1955, pp. 21-22 and pp. 86-87; S. M. Imaduddin: "Bayt al-Mal and Banks in the Medieval Muslim World," in *Islamic Culture,* Vol. 34, Hyderabad, 1960, pp. 22-30; and the elaborate bibliography in my article "Djahbadh" in *Encylopaedia of Islam,* n.ed. 1962, Vol. II, pp. 382-383.

20. Attention should be drawn to some valuable and relevant comments and suggestions made in various studies and reviews of this book, such as A. Cohen: "Die Wirtschaftliche Stellung der Juden in Bagdad im 10. Jahrhundert, Ein Beitrag zur Frage des historischen Anteils der Juden am Wirtschaftsleben," *Mon. f. d. Gesch. u. Wiss. d. Judentums,* Breslau, 1935, pp. 361-381; Charles C. Torrey: "The Evolution of a Financier in the Ancient Near East," *Journal of Near Eastern Studies,* Chicago, 1943, Vol. II, No. 4, pp. 295-301; Jacob Mann in *Tarbitz,*" Jerusalem, 1935, Vol. V, pp. 148-179; and Salo W. Baron: *A Social and Religious History of the Jews,* Vol. III pp. 304 ff., see also M. Canard in his French translation of the Arabic text of Muhammad b. Yahyā as-Sūlī: "Akhbār Ar-Rādī Billāh wa'l-Muttaqī billāh," in *Publications de l'Institut D'Études Orientales de la Faculté des Lettres d'Alger,* Algiers, 1946 and 1950, 2 Vols.

21. While no additional new data have come forth in regards to the Jewish Vizier, Ya'qūb b. Killis, valuable information on the Banū Sahl and their relationship to the Jewish communities and on other economic aspects, such as "jahbadh" and "suftaja" could be derived from the Judeo-Arabic fragments of the Cairo Geniza. See S. D.

Goitein: *A Mediterranean Society,* Vol. I, Economic Foundations, Los Angeles-Berkeley, 1967, pp. 242-254 and his study in *Tarbitz,* Jerusalem, 1967, Vol. 36, p. 368 ff. The published Geniza fragments, relevant to the Banū Sahl, are listed in Shaul Shaked: *A Tentative Bibliography of Geniza Documents (up to 1963),* Paris, The Hague, 1964.

22. In an effort to find allusions to Sa'd ad-Daula in contemporary Hebrew sources, Abraham Ben-Jacob has made various suggestions which, however, do not seem plausible. See his *A History of the Jews in Iraq from the End of the Gaonic Period 1038 C.E. to the Present Time,* Ben-Zvi Institute, Hebrew University, Jerusalem, 1965, pp. 57-69.

23. The rather short sketch given on pp. 122-125 was supplemented immediately after the appearance of this book in my study: "Über Raschid ad-Daula's Juedischen Ursprung" in *Mon. f. d. Gesch. u. Wiss. d. Judentums,* Breslau, 1937, pp. 144-153; for a more elaborate survey, see my article "Azarbaijan in Jewish History" in *Proceedings of the American Academy of Jewish Research,* New York, 1953, pp. 11-21, where most of the Arabic and Persian sources have been listed.

24. Karl Jahn of the University of Leiden has devoted all his energy to the edition and translation of Rashīd ad-Dīn's *Universal History* for which the scholarly world is greatly indebted to him.

See his edition of Rashīd ad-Dīn's "History of Ghāzān" in *Gibb Memorial Series,* n.s., London, 1940; *Ta'rīh-i-Mubārak-i-Gāzānī (Geschichte der Ilhāne Abāga bis Gaihātū, 1265-1295),* ed. Prag, 1941; *Histoire Universelle de Rasid Al-Din Fadl Allāh Abul-Kair, Histiore des Francs,* Leiden, 1951; *Rashīd al-Dīn's History of India, Collected Essays,* the Hague, 1965; see also his study "Rashīd ad-Dīn as World Historian" in *Yadnaze-ye Jan Rypka,* Prag, 1967, pp. 79-87.

25. Most of these Arabic and Persian sources have been listed in my study "Azarbaijan in Jewish History," in *Proceedings of the American Academy of Jewish Research,* New York, 1953, pp. 11-21.

26. He was one of the victims of a wave of conversions which swept over the intellectual strata of Babylonian-Persian Jewry in the second part of the 13th century. The Jewish philosopher of Baghdād, Sa'd b. Manṣūr Ibn Kammūna (d. 1284) (see about him above, pp. 134-136) raised his voice against these conversions in his

philosophical work entitled *Examination of the Inquiries into the Three Faiths, A 13th Century Essay in Comparative Religion,* now available in its complete Arabic text ed. by Moshe Perlmann; *Near Eastern Studies,* Los Angeles-Berkeley, 1967, Vol. 6.

27. The 12th-century traveler, Benjamin of Tudela, estimated in his *Travels* the size of the Jewish community in Hamadan at about 50,000—a figure which is evidently grossly exaggerated. The *Igroth of R. Samuel b. Eli* (ed. Assaf, Jerusalem, 1930, pp. 28-29) informs us that in the first half of the 13th century, Hamadan was an important cultural center, a seat of a well-organized Jewish community with a Yeshivah, in close contact with the Talmudic academies in Baghdad.

28. An English translation of his *History of the Children of Israel* is in preparation by the writer.

29. On Ibn Khaldūn's knowledge of Judaism, see my study "Ibn Khaldūn: On the Bible, Judaism and the Jews" in Ignace Goldziher *Memorial Volume, Part II,* Jerusalem, 1956, pp. 147-171, and my recent book *Ibn Khaldūn in Egypt: His Public Functions and His Historical Research,* Los Angeles-Berkeley, 1967, pp. 138-155.

30. See Reuben Levy, *Persian Literature,* London, 1923, pp. 67-68.

31. We deemed it relevant, though our major theme here is economic-centered, to mention that the same cultural climate which had enabled such Court Jews as Sa'd ad-Daula and Rashīd ad-Daula to make their contribution to the economic and political sphere, led also to the genesis and growth of the Judeo-Persian literature, that branch of literary efforts, cultivated exclusively by the Persian Jews from the 13th and 14th centuries on.

This passing reference (pp. 124-125) has meanwhile been substantiated by a number of monographs and studies which tried to explore in greater depth the Judeo-Persian productivity starting with the 14th century Shāhīn of Shirāz, the translation of the Bible into the Judeo-Persian language and the transliteration of classical Persian poetry into the Judeo-Persian script and other literary expressions of the creative spirit of Persian Jewry.

See my studies: "Israel in Iran, A Survey of Judeo-Persian Literature," in *The Jews, Their History, Culture and Religion,* ed. L. Finkelstein, 3rd ed., New York, 1960, pp. 1149-1190; "The Bible in Persian Translation" in *Harvard Theological Review,* 1952, Vol. 45, pp. 3-45; "The Beginnings of Judeo-Persian Literature" in *Mélanges d'Orientalisme offerts à H. Masse,* Teheran, 1963, pp. 141-

150, and *Jewish Book Annual,* New York, Vol. 27, 1969.

See also Jan Rypka, *History of the Iranian Literature,* ed. Karl Jahn, Dordrecht, Holland, 1968, pp. 737-740; and the valuable articles in *Studies in Bibliography and Booklore,* Cincinnati, 1968, Vol. 8, No. 224, pp. 43-136, dedicated to Judeo-Persian studies.

32. After the death of Rashīd ad-Daula, the sources confront us with but one other Jewish personality, apparently of great prominence, called "a pillar of the Jewish community in Baghdād", Manṣūr b. Abi'l Harūn (about 1333) whose honorific title, Sadīd ad-Daula, would indicate his public standing in the Islamic administration, toward the end of the Il-Khān rule. It seems that this Sadīd ad-Daula was the last manifestation of the phenomenon of Court Jews in the 14th century of Eastern Islam.

See Abu'l-Fidā: *Ta'rīkh,* Vol. IV, p. 113; adh-Dhahabī: *Duwal al-Islām,* Vol. II, p. 187, and my article in *Mon. f. d. Gesch, u. Wiss. d. Judentums,* Breslau, 1937, Vol. 81, pp. 418-422, where the sources are detailed.

33. The abundance of source material pertaining to the Court Jews during the Ottoman rule has hardly yet been utilized for Jewish economic history. For the role of Court Jews in the Asiatic provinces of the Ottoman Empire in the 19th century, see *The Travels of Rabbi David d'Beth Hillel, from Jerusalem through Arabia, Koordistan, Part of Persia and India to Madras,* Madras, 1832; and my article: "The Jews of Kurdistan One Hundred Years Ago," in *Jewish Social Studies,* New York, 1944, Vol. VI, pp. 195-226, based on it.

34. See p. 28 and also p. 59 in the text.

35. The institution of the Court Jew in a different form, however, was prevalent also in 17th and 18th-century India when leading Jews, as merchants, negotiators, interpreters and diplomats, were serving the "Courts" of the Commanders or Governors of the various East India Companies—the Portuguese, the Dutch, the English—in Bombay, Goa, Cochin, Surat, Calcutta etc.

For this aspect, see my book *The Jews of India: Their Contribution to the Economic and Political Life from the 16th Century On,* Ben Zvi Institute, Hebrew University, Jerusalem, 1960, and my more comprehensive volume on this topic in English, soon to appear.

PREFACE

THE manifold relations between the various branches of Islamic and Jewish literature during the Middle Ages have long been the subject of research by eminent scholars such as A. Geiger, M. Steinschneider, I. Friedländer, I. Goldziher, etc. Corresponding relationships in the field of economic and political life, however, have hitherto not had sufficient attention devoted to them. It is possible that the latter relationships were overlooked because of the *ahl adh-Dhimma* provisions in Islamic law, known in Europe mostly by the works of Abū Yūsuf and al-Māwardi, according to which non-Muslims were excluded from all public services.

But that was only in theory. The numerous edicts disqualifying Christians and Jews from administrative posts, which were so often re-enacted by successive Caliphs, are symptomatic of the imperfect application of the theory, and show that daily life followed rules far different from those which jurists and theologians laid down.

The following study, based on a systematic investigation of the Arabic historical sources, attempts to indicate the part actually played by Jews in the economic and political spheres of some Islamic countries such as 'Irāq, Egypt, and Persia during the period between the tenth and the thirteenth centuries.

The material, scattered throughout the Arabic literature and offered here, centres round a number of outstanding personalities. They are mostly border-line figures linking the worlds of Judaism and Islam, who, favoured by a ruler or some other historical circumstances, were called upon, in virtue of their abilities and service, to take an active part in the public life of their time, thus affecting the course of general history. They show the familiar career of a sudden rise and an equally sudden end, common to so many other prominent individuals in Eastern autocracies.

It is not the result of arbitrary choice that we deal here only with leading Jews. This is caused by the attitude of the Arabic authors, who in general refer very sparingly to non-Muslims, mentioning only those amongst them who were accorded special interest by reason of their position and activities. Had this not been so, our information regarding the economic situation of the Jews in Mediaeval Islam might have been somewhat more complete.

It should be remarked that the starting-point of our inquiry has been the Islamic sources available. Continued research into hitherto unpublished sources will doubtless produce additional information and serve to fill the lacunæ in the history of Oriental Jewry. Hebrew documents and records, dealing mostly with the inner religious life of the Jewish community, have been utilized when they had a direct bearing upon our subject.

The background of our study extends from Egypt to Persia during the Middle Ages. Though the terms "Middle Ages" or "Mediaeval", taken over from European history, are scarcely exact in this connection, they are retained here as a matter of convenience. The similar problems of Jewry at other periods and under Islamic dynasties in other countries such as Spain, North Africa, Turkey, etc., are reserved for a separate work.

In conclusion I wish to thank Professor D. S. Margoliouth (Oxford) for his valuable suggestions and guidance; Colonel D. M. F. Hoysted for ensuring the publication of this book by the Royal Asiatic Society and for his good offices; I. M. Lask for his help in revising the English version; Dr. S. D. Goitein and I. A. Abbady for reading the proof-sheets.

WALTER J. FISCHEL.

HEBREW UNIVERSITY,
JERUSALEM.

March, 1936.

SOURCES

ABU'L-FIDĀ'. *Annales Muslemici*, ed. Reiske, Hafniae, 1788/1793.

ABŪ YŪSUF. *Kitāb al-Kharāj*, Būlāq, 1302.

'ARĪB B. SA'D. *Ṭabari continuatus*, ed. de Goeje, Leyden, 1897.

BAR HEBRÆUS. *Chronicon Syriacum*, ed. P. Bedjan, Paris, 1890.
The Chronography of Gregory Bar Hebræus Abu'l Faraj, ed. and transl. by E. A. W. Budge, London, 1932.
Mukhtaṣar, ed. Salhani, Beyrouth, 1890.

ADH-DHAHABI. *Kitāb Duwal al-Islām*, Ḥyderābād, 1337.

ECL. = *The Eclipse of the 'Abbasid Caliphate*, ed. and transl. by H. F. Amedroz and D. S. Margoliouth, Oxford, 1921.

GHĀZI B. AL-WĀSIṬI. *Ar-radd 'ala Ahl adh-Dhimma*, ed. R. Gottheil, *JAOS.*, 1921, vol. 41.

AL-HAMADHĀNI. Takmilat-Ta'rīkh aṭ-Ṭabari MS., Paris, No. 1469.

HAMDULLAH MUSTAWFĪ-I QAZWĪNI. *Ta'rīkh-i Guzīda*, ed. E. G. Browne, London, 1910 (Gibb Memor. Vol. xiv).

—— *Nuzhat al-Qulūb*, ed. Le Strange, London, 1915 (Gibb. Mem. Vol. xxiii).

HILĀL AṢ-ṢĀBI. *Kitāb al Wuzarā'*, ed. Amedroz, Leyden, 1904.

IBN ABĪ UṢAIBI'A. *Ṭabaqāt al-Aṭibbā'*, ed. Müller, Königsberg, 1884.

IBN AL-ATHĪR. *Chronicon*, ed. Tornberg, Leyden, 1867/1874.

IBN BAṬŪṬA. *Voyages*, ed. C. Defrémery et B. Sanguinetti, Paris, 1843/1922

IBN DUQMĀQ. *Description de l'Égypte*, ed. Vollers, Cairo, 1893.

IBN AL-FAKĪH. *Kitāb al-Buldān*, ed. de Goeje, Leyden, 1885 (*Bibl. Geogr. Arab.*, v).

IBN AL-FUWAṬI. *al-Ḥawādith al-Jāmi'a wa-t-Tajārib an-Nāfi'a*, Baghdād, 1351/1932, ed. M. Jawād.

IBN AL-ḤAUQAL. *Kitāb al-Masālik wa-l-Mamālik*, ed. de Goeje, Leyden, 1873 (*Bibl. Geogr. Arab.*, ii).

IBN IYĀS. *Kitāb Ta'rīkh Miṣr*, Būlāq, 1311.

IBN KHALDŪN. *Prolegomena*, ed. E. Quatremère, Paris, 1859 (*Notices et Extraits*, xvi).

IBN KHALLIKĀN. *Wafayāt al-A'yān*, Būlāq, 1275.

IBN KHURDĀDHBEH. *Kitāb al-Masālik wa'l-Mamālik*, ed. de Goeje, Leyden, 1889 (*Bibl. Geogr. Arab.*, vi).

IBN AL-MU'TAZZ. *Dīwān*, ed. C. Lang, *ZDMG.*, 1886/1887.

IBN MUYASSAR. *Akhbār Miṣr*, ed. H. Massé, Cairo, 1919.

IBN AN-NAQQĀSH. *Fetoua relatif à la condition des Zimmis . . .*, ed. M. Belin, *Journ. Asiat.*, 1851/1852.

IBN AL-QALĀNISI. *Dhail Ta'rīkh Dimashq*, ed. Amedroz, Leyden, 1908.

IBN AL- ṬI. *Ta'rīkh al-Ḥukamā'*, ed. Lippert, Leipzig, 1903.

IBN ROSTEH. *Kitāb al-A'lāq an-Nafīsa*, ed. de Goeje, Leyden, 1892 (*Bibl. Geogr. Arab.*, vii).

IBN AS-SĀ'I. *al-Jāmi' al-Mukhtaṣar*, Baghdād, 1353/1934, ed. M. Jawād and Père Anastase al-Karmeli.

IBN SA'ĪD. *Kitāb al-Mughrib*, ed. L. Tallquist, Leyden, 1897.

IBN AṢ-ṢAIRAFI. *al-Ishāra ilā man nāla-l-Wizāra*, ed. A. Mukhliṣ, Cairo, 1924.

IBN TAGHRIBIRDI. *an-Nujūm aẓ-Ẓāhira*, ed. Juynboll, Leiden, 1852/1857. ed. W. Popper, Berkeley, 1909 ff.

AL-IṢṬAKHRI. *Kitāb Masālik al-Mamālik*, ed. de Goeje, Leyden, 1927 (*Bibl. Geogr. Arab.*, i).

AL-JĀḤIẒ. *Kitāb al-Ḥayawān*, Cairo, 1325.

—— *Thalāth Rasā'il*, ed. J. Finkel, Cairo, 1344.

AL-JAHSHIYĀRI. *Kitāb al-Wuzarā'*, ed. v. Mžik, Leipzig, 1926.

KHALĪL AẒ-ẒĀHIRI. *Kitāb Zubdat Kashf al-Mamālik*, ed. P. Ravaisse, Paris, 1894.

KHWĀNDAMĪR. *Ḥabību's-Siyar*, Bombay, 1857.

AL-KHWĀRIZMI. *Mafātīḥ al-'Ulūm*, ed. v. Vloten, Leyden, 1895.

AL-KINDI. *Governors and Judges of Egypt*, ed. Rh. Guest, London, 1912 (Gibb Mem. Vol. xix).

AL-KUTUBI. *Fawāt al-Wafayāt*, Būlāq, 1283.

LEROY, L. *Histoire d'Abraham le Syrien, Patriarche copte d'Alexandrie*, Paris, 1909/1910 (*Revue de l'Orient Chrétien*).

AL-MAQRĪZI. *al-Khiṭaṭ wa-l-Āthār*, Būlāq, 1270. This work is always meant, unless otherwise stated.

—— *Itti'āẓ al-Ḥunafā'*, ed. H. Bunz, Leipzig, 1909.

—— *Shudhūr al-'Uqūd*, ed. L. A. Mayer, Alexandria, 1933.

AL-MAS'ŪDI. *Kitāb at-Tanbīh wa-l-Ishrāf*, ed. de Goeje, Leyden, 1894 (*Bibl. Geogr. Arab.*, viii).

AL-MĀWARDI. *Constitutiones Politicae*, ed. M. Enger, Bonn, 1853.

AL-MISKAWAIH. *Kitāb Tajārib al-Umam*, ed. and transl. by Amedroz and Margoliouth, Oxford, 1920 (in *The Eclipse of the 'Abbasid Caliphate*).

AL-MUBARRAD. *Kāmil*, ed. W. Wright, Leipzig, 1864.

MUFAḌḌAL B. ABI'L-FAḌĀ'IL. *Histoire des Sultans Mamlouks*, ed. Blochet, Paris, 1919/1929 (*Patrolog. Orient.*, vols. xii, xiv, xx).

AL-MUQADDASI. *Descriptio Imperii Moslemici*, ed. de Goeje, Leyden, 1906 (*Bibl. Arab. Geogr.*, iii).

NĀṢIR-I-KHOSRAU. *Sefer Nāmeh*, ed. et trad. Ch. Schefer, Paris, 1881.

AN-NUWAIRI. *Nihāyat al-Arab fī Funūn al-Adab MS. Leyden No.* 5 (*Cat. Cod. Orient. Bibl.*, i, pp. 4/5, ed. Dozy, Leyden, 1851).

AL-QALQASHANDI. *Ṣubḥ al-A'shā*, Cairo, 1913/1922.

QUDĀMA B. JA'FAR. *Kitāb al-Kharāj*, MS. Paris, No. 5907.

RASHĪD AD-DĪN. *Jāmi' at-Tawārīkh*, MS. Add. 16688 British Museum.

SA'ĪD B. ḤASAN. *Kitāb Masālik an-Naẓar*, ed. S. A. Weston, *JAOS.*, 1903.

AṢ-ṢŪLI. *Adab al-Kuttāb*, Baghdād, 1341.

—— *Akhbār ar-Rāḍi wa-l-Muttaqi from the Kitāb al-Awrāq*, ed. J. Heyworth Dunne, London, 1935.

AS-SUYŪṬI. *Ḥusn al-Muḥāḍara*, Cairo, 1299.

AṬ-ṬABARI. *Annales*, ed. de Goeje, Leyden, 1879 ff.

AT-TANŪKHI. *Nishwār al-Muḥāḍara*, ed. D. S. Margoliouth; vol. i, London, 1922; vol. ii, Damascus, 1930. Transl. vol. i, London, 1923; vol. ii, Ḥyderābād, 1931.

—— *al-Faraj ba'd ash-Shidda*, Cairo, 1903/1904.

WAṢṢĀF. *'Abdullah b. Faḍlullah of Shīrāẓ : Ta'rīkh-i-Waṣṣāf*, MS. Brit. Mus., Add. 23517. The lithograph edition, Bombay, 1852, was inaccessible to me.

YAḤYĀ B. SA'ĪD. *Annales*, ed. L. Cheikho, Beyrouth, 1909 ; ed. F. Kratchkovsky and A. Vasiliev, Paris, 1924, 1932 (*Patrol. Orient.*, vols. xviii, xxiii).

YĀQŪT. *Irshād al-Arīb*, ed. D. S. Margoliouth, London, 1907/1913 (Gibb Mem. Vol. vi).

—— *Mu'jam al-Buldān*, ed. F. Wüstenfeld, Göttingen, 1866 ff.

ZETTERSTÉEN, K. V. *Beiträge zur Geschichte der Mamlukensultane nach arab. Handschriften*, Leyden, 1919.

PERIODICALS

Enc. Isl. = *Encyclopædia of Islam.*
Enc. Jud. = *Encyclopædia Judaica.*
JA. = *Journal Asiatique.*
JAOS. = *Journal of the American Oriental Society.*
JQR. = *Jewish Quarterly Review.*
JRAS. = *Journal of the Royal Asiatic Society.*
MGWJ. = *Monatsschrift für Geschichte und Wissenschaft des Judentums.*
MSOS. = *Mitteilungen des Seminars für Orientalische Sprachen, Berlin.*
REJ. = *Revue des Etudes Juives.*
ZDMG. = *Zeitschrift der Deutschen Morgenländischen Gesellschaft.*

A. UNDER THE 'ABBĀSID CALIPHATE [1]

1

THE last few decades have seen the publication of several hitherto unedited Arab sources relative to the history of the 'Abbāsid Empire in the tenth century, such as *Kitāb al-Wuzarā'* by Hilāl aṣ-Ṣābi,[2] *Kitāb Tajārib al-Umam* by Miskawaih,[3] and *Nishwār al-Muḥāḍara* by at-Tanūkhi,[4] that are a veritable storehouse of information on the social, economic, and political situation of that period. These works reveal a completely new world to us; they take us, so to speak, behind the scenes of tenth century 'Abbāsid administration and we observe the entire governmental machinery in action.

This is chiefly due to the historiographical approach of the authors [5]; themselves high government officials, they dwell particularly on economic and administrative details, and are keenly interested in financial affairs, the system of farming revenue, the management of estates, the bureaucratic

[1] The material offered in this chapter was published in a slightly different form in the *JRAS.*, 1933, pp. 339 ff., 569 ff., under the title "The Origin of Banking in Mediaeval Islam: A Contribution to the economic history of the Jews of Baghdād in the tenth century."

[2] Abbreviated *Wuz.*

[3] Abbrev. *Misk.*

[4] Abbrev. *Tan.* See now also *aṣ-Ṣūli: Akhbār ar-Rāḍi*, London, 1935.

[5] Regarding the place occupied by these writers in Arab historiography, cf. the various editors' prefaces; further D. S. Margoliouth, *Arabic Historians*, Calcutta, 1930, pp. 128–137; the corresponding articles in the *Enc. Isl.*; Amedroz in *Der Islam*, ii (1911), pp. 105–114; ibid., v (1914), pp. 335–357; M. Hartmann, "Aus der Gesellschaft des verfallenden Abbasidenreiches," *Le Monde Oriental*, iii, 1909, pp. 247–266.

apparatus, the viziers and their actions. These sources for the administration of the 'Abbāsid empire contain a vast number of names and titles of various institutions, departments, and offices, all representing parts of the administrative network which we see functioning. But we do not immediately perceive how all those institutions work and, by mutual effort, bring about the resultant effect; neither do we see what function corresponds to each section of this governmental machine.

In order to find the way through this administrative maze, one method alone is advisable: to start from the *terminology*, investigating each term or title separately.[1] In a primeval forest the uprooting of a single tree, with all its entanglements and ramifications, may open a way to a clearing; and similarly the analysis of a particular expression, and its thorough elucidation, may help to disentangle a whole skein of concepts.

The Concept of a Jahbadh

As a starting-point for our inquiry we may conveniently choose the concept of *jahbadh* (جَهْبَذ), a term in frequent use. Tāj al-'Arūs [2] paraphrases this term in a general way as "a money expert, experienced in most intricate affairs, very well versed in matters of cash". Dozy [3] renders the expression with "vérificateur, changeur", Karabacek [4]

[1] According to this method, the expressions بيت مال الخاصّة and بيت مال العامّة, that occur so frequently in these sources, have been dealt with in a separate paper. Cf. *Oriente Moderno*, Rome, 1936, p. 104, and *JRAS.*, 1936.

[2] *Tāj al-'Arūs*, ii, p. 555.

[3] Dozy, *Supplément*, i, p. 225 s.v., reads also *jihbadh* (جِهْبِذ), pl. جهابذة. The word *jahbadh* is supposed to be of Persian origin. Cf. Vullers, *Lexicon Persicum*, i, p. 544, s.v. كهبد, *exactor vectigalium*.

[4] *Mitteilungen aus der Sammlung der Papyrus Erzherzog Rainer*, Wien, 1887, vol. ii, p. 169.

with "Saeckelwart", v. Kremer [1] with "Regierungskassierer", Wahrmund [2] with "ein guter Geldkenner, ein geschickter Wechsler", Amedroz [3] with "treasury receiver", D. S. Margoliouth [4] with "collector", A. Mez [5] with "Bankier", and L. Massignon [6] likewise with "banquier". [7]

A bearer of this title, *jahbadh*, is already mentioned in Arab sources of the time of al-Manṣūr (754–775). [8] But persons so designated become more frequent only in the tenth century. This fact is probably connected with the flourishing state of commerce at this period and the changed basis of its general economic structure. Towards the end of the ninth century a change took place in the financial administration of the ʿAbbāsid empire; this, as v. Kremer has already pointed out, [9] was due to the replacement of the silver (*dirham*) standard, hitherto used in Islamic state economy, by the gold (*dīnār*) standard. It is noteworthy that in the tax-rolls of the eighth and ninth centuries [10] the revenues of the western provinces

[1] *Ueber das Einnahmebudget des Abbasidenreiches*, Wien, 1887, p. 8.

[2] *Handwoerterbuch der arabischen und deutschen Sprache*, Giessen, 1887, i, p. 464.

[3] Glossary to his edition of *Kitāb al-wuzarā'*, p. 59. Cf., however, *JRAS.* 1908, p. 432, "receiving clerk."

[4] In his translations of *Misk.* and *Tan.*

[5] *Die Renaissance des Islam*, Heidelberg, 1922, p. 450.

[6] "L'influence de l'Islam au moyen âge sur la fondation et l'essor des banques juives" (*Bulletin d'Etudes Orientales de l'Institut Français de Damas*, 1932).

[7] For the translation of this expression by "banker" cf. also de Sacy, *Chrestomatie Arabe*, Paris, 1806, ii, p. 330. It is justified by the actual functions of the *jahbadh* which we really know only now from the new sources. The banking function of the *jahbadh* only developed in the tenth century from sorting and trading in coins. The evolution from money-changer to money-lender and banker is a phenomenon that has also been observed in other civilizations. Vide M. Weber, *Wirtschaftsgeschichte*, München, 1923, p. 226; *Handw. d. Staatswissenschaften*, s.v. *Banken*; Kulischer, *Warenhändler und Geldausleiher im Mittelalter*, *Zeitschrift für Volkswirtschaft und Verwaltung*, vol. 17 (1908), p. 218.

[8] al-Jahshiyāri, op. cit., p. 53*a*, l. 9, 11; p. 63*a*, l. 5.

[9] Op. cit., pp. 6 ff.

[10] These tax-rolls, upon which A. v. Kremer based his study of the financial administration in his still valuable *Kulturgeschichte des Orients*, Wien, 1875,

are stated in gold, and those of the eastern ones in silver. In a tenth century budget, on the other hand, all the items are already expressed in gold.[1] These new currency conditions, as well as the diversity of coins in circulation and their fluctuating relative values, necessitated the conversion of coins received by the public exchequer; and it was just this conversion that was performed by the *jahbadh*. The *jahbadh's* function accordingly became an indispensable one, and his increasing importance is most clearly manifested by three facts: (*a*) repeated reference to the *māl al-jahbadha*; (*b*) the establishing of a special *Dīwān al-jahbadha*; and (*c*) the frequent mention of bearers of the title of *jahbadh* by name.

The *māl al-jahbadha* is a sort of tax, a premium or exchange rate that played a considerable part in the financial life of those times. As a special item it appears in the income budget for the years 918/919.[2] In *Hilāl aṣ-Ṣābi* we again come across the *māl al-jahbadha* as an integral part of the public income, and the discussion in which it is mentioned gives us for the first time valuable information as to its real nature.[3] We learn there that 'Ali b. 'Īsā, later so famous as a Vizier,[4] had to draw up an estimate of the revenues of the Mosul and Zāb district when he was the head of the Dīwān ad-Dār. His principal, Abu 'l-'Abbās b. al-Furāt, the brother of the Vizier Ḥasan b. al-Furāt, found on examining this budget scheme that the *māl al-jahbadha* had not been included as an item. 'Ali b. 'Īsā, however, replied that he desired to be fair in his

i, pp. 256–379, and in *Verhandlungen des VII. Internat. Oriental. Kongresses*, Wien, 1886, pp. 1–18, are to be found (in chronological order): (*a*) Ibn Khaldūn, Muqaddima, vol. xvi, pp. 321–4; (*b*) al-Jahshiyāri, pp. 179*b*–182*b*; (*c*) Qudāma b. Ja'far, pp. 236–252; (*d*) Ibn Khurdādhbeh, pp. 8 ff.

[1] The Arab geographers and other Arab sources contain many references to the variety of coins and their respective values. The collection of this material toward a monetary history of the Islamic peoples is a desideratum.

[2] Kremer, *Einnahmebudget*, pp. 28, 32, 34, 38.

[3] Cf. also H. F. Amedroz, "Abbasid Administration in its Decay," *JRAS.*, 1913, p. 835; *Wuz.*, 255.

[4] Regarding him see the meritorious work of H. Bowen, *The Life and Times of 'Ali ibn 'Isā*, Cambridge, 1928.

treatment of the taxpayers and not impose the money-changer's profit upon the subjects of this newly conquered province. Nevertheless, Abu 'l-'Abbās b. al-Furāt insisted upon the registration of this exchange rate [1] as a special item of the revenue. Later we hear of a certain 'Īsā an-naqqād,[2] who was placed in charge of the *māl al-jahbadha*.

The establishment of a special *dīwān al-jahbadha* is first reported in the year 928,[3] and as its head is mentioned a Christian, Ibrāhīm b. Ayyūb. In Qudāma b. Ja'far's *Kitāb al-Kharāj* the institution of a *Dīwān al-jahbadha* is discussed in detail, and full particulars are given of the affairs which it conducted.[4]

But the part played by the *jahbadha* is revealed not only by the coming into use of *māl al-jahbadha* as a fixed term of tenth century Islamic financial administration, and by the institution of a Dīwān. Our sources also mention bearers of the title of *jahbadha* by name, and even give us fairly precise information as to their activities. We thus hear, e.g., of a *jahbadh* named Ibrāhīm b. Aḥmad b. Idrīs,[5] of one Ibrāhīm b. Yūḥannā,[6] of a Zakariyyā b. Yūḥannā,[7] of Sahl b. Naẓīr,[8] of Isrā'īl b. Ṣāliḥ,[9] of Nikolas b Andūna,[10] of Merkūr b. Shanūda,[11] etc.,[12] and last, but not least, of two Jewish bearers of the title.

[1] Further evidence for *māl al-jahbadha* v. *Wuz.*, 291; *Ecl.*, iii, 71. Cf. also A. Harkavy, *Studien und Mitteilungen*, Berlin, 1887, pp. 274, 340, 364. See also *Maqrīzi*, i, 272, and A. Grohmann, "Probleme der Arabischen Papyrusforschung," *Archiv Orientalni*, Praha v, 273–283; vi, 125–149.

[2] *Wuz.*, 291; v. also *Wuz.*, 224.

[3] *'Arīb*, 135.

[4] MS. Paris, No. 5907, fol. 23*a–b*; Mez, op. cit., p. 72, calls this Dīwān "Reichsbank", which, however, is much too modern.

[5] *Wuz.*, 224.

[6] *Wuz.*, 226; *Misk.*, 95, 99.

[7] *Wuz.*, 158.

[8] *Misk.*, 349, 379.

[9] *Misk.*, 349, 11, 52.

[10] In a papyrus of the tenth century, ed. by D. S. Margoliouth, in "Select Arabic Papyri of the Rylands Collection" in *Florilegium M. de Vogué*, Paris, 1909, pp. 416–17. Here the *jahbadh* receives the Kharāj.

[11] In an eleventh century payrus, ed. by Karabacek, loc. cit.

[12] Cf. *Ibn Rosteh*, p. 207. *Vide* also Gottheil-Worrell, *Geniza Fragments*, New York, 1927, pp. 70–1 and 164–5.

The Position of the Ahl adh-Dhimma under al-Muqtadir

None of the bearers of the *jahbadha* title seems to have played a part at the Caliph al-Muqtadir's court equal to that of these two Jewish bankers, whose names were *Joseph b. Phineas* [1] and *Aaron b. Amram*.[2] This surprising fact leads us to the problem of Jewish officials in 'Abbāsid times. The Caliphs, in spite of all restrictions *de jure*, actually found themselves quite unable to dispense with the particular abilities of the *ahl adh-Dhimma* for certain professions, and were thus obliged to admit them into the ranks of their civil service.[3] The Caliph al-Muqtadir, too, whose reign is the only one with which we are here concerned, could not help admitting Jews and Christians to certain governmental functions. Even before his time [4] there must have been non-Muslim civil servants, for he had to regulate anew the question of the *ahl adh-Dhimma* as administrative officials at the very

[1] *Wuz.*, 79, 80, 158, 178; *'Arīb*, 74; *Tan.*, ii, 81 ff. يوسف بن فينحاس الجهبذ اليهودى, sometimes فيجاس.

[2] *Wuz.*, 33, 79, 80, 124, 158, 306–7; *Misk.*, 79–80, 112, 128; *'Arīb*, 74, 91; *Tan.*, ii, 81 ff. Cf. also *Misk.*, 44, 66. هارون بن عمران الجهبذ اليهودى.

[3] See A. S. Tritton, *The Caliphs and their non-Muslim Subjects*, London, 1930; and a further article by the same author in *JRAS.*, April, 1931, pp. 311–338. A. Mez, loc. cit., pp. 28–55. See also Yūsuf R. Ghanīma, *Ta'rīkh Yahūd al 'Irāq*, Baghdād, 1924. Cf. I. Goldziher, Usages Juifs d'après la littérature religieuse des Musulmans, *REJ.*, vol. xxviii (1894), pp. 75–94; the "Appendice", pp. 91 ff., is especially instructive, though concerned with later times. Cf. *Ibn an-Naqqāsh*, ed. Belin, and *Ghāzi b. al-Wāsiṭi*, ed. Gottheil.

[4] During the reign of the Caliph al-Mu'taḍid numerous Jews and Christians again became government officials. The Vizier 'Ubaidallah b. Sulaymān, in a reply to the Caliph, justifies this measure as follows: "Not because of any sympathy on my part for Judaism or Christianity did I take the Unbelievers into civil service, but because I found them to be more faithfully attached to thy dynasty than Muslims." Cited by H. Graetz, *Geschichte d. Juden*, vol. v, p. 277, from a passage in J. J. Assemani's *Bibliotheca Orientalis Clementino-Vaticana*, Rome, 1719–1728, vol. iii, pars 2.

beginning of his reign. In 908 [1] he promulgated an edict admitting Jews and Christians to two state functions only; those, namely, of physician and of banker جهبذة. It is extremely significant that he did not desire to exclude Jews and Christians from all administrative posts, but only to define the offices to which they were restricted. In so doing he was probably legalizing the *status quo*, while taking into consideration the needs of the State.

The extent of Jewish participation in these two official functions left open to them by the State could hitherto be inferred only from a single reference in the work of the Arab geographer al-Muqaddasi.[2] In describing the situation in Egypt and Syria he says: "Most bankers, dyers, money-changers, and tanners here are Jews [3]; most medical men and clerks are Christians." [4]

[1] Strangely enough, neither Ṭabari nor Ibn al-Athīr mention this edict; the only evidence is Ibn Taghribirdi's work, *An-Nujūm az-Zāhira*, ed. T. G. Juynboll, vol. ii, p. 174. The text reads as follows:—

امر المقتدر ان لا يستخدم احد اليهود والنصارى الا فى الطبّ والجهبذة فقط

According to this edict, Jews and Christians were also subjected again to limitations of attire; but it is improbable that the latter were strictly enforced. ʿ*Arīb*, 30, mentions a particular prohibition directed against Christians in the civil service.

[2] Ed. de Goeje, p. 183, l. 6.

واكثر الجهابذة والصبّاغين والصيارفة والدبّاغين بهذا الاقليم يهود؛

واكثر الاطبّاء والكتبة نصارى

The new sources show that this distribution of occupations existed simultaneously not only in Syria and Egypt but also in Babylonia. For the earlier period cf. Abū Yūsuf, *Kitāb al-kharāj*, pp. 70–1.

[3] This statement, however, applies only to the end of the ninth and the beginning of the tenth century. We learn from the recently published treatise ردّ على النصارى of al-Jāḥiẓ, ed. J. Finkel, that at the time of the Caliph al-Mutawakkil (847–861) the Babylonian Jews were dyers, tanners, barbers, butchers, etc., while the Christians held socially higher positions, being money-changers, secretaries, court attendants, medical men, druggists, etc. Cf. D. S. Margoliouth, ʿAli b. Rabbān aṭ-Ṭabari's Book of Religion (*Proceedings of the British Academy*, xvi, 1930, p. 173). *Vide*, however, al-Jāḥiẓ, *Kitāb al-ḥayawān*, vol. v, p. 52, where Jews are praised because of their sincerity—perhaps as bankers, as Professor Margoliouth suggests. In the course of the tenth century a considerable change must have taken place in the professional composition

The evidence of the geographer Muqaddasi, together with the edict of the Caliph al-Muqtadir, have hitherto been the only direct statements we possessed concerning the occupations of the Jews in the tenth century 'Abbāsid empire. Our new sources not only confirm these statements but also supplement them considerably. The data now in our possession actually show two Jews, Joseph b. Phineas and Aaron b. Amram, in the performance of their *jahbadh* functions, and the part they were able to play in virtue of those functions at the court of the Caliph al-Muqtadir. To these Jewish bankers we will now direct our attention.

Titles ; Internal Organization ; Time

Joseph b. Phineas and Aaron b. Amram are repeatedly mentioned in the sources as *al-jahbadhān al-yahūdiyyān*, the two Jewish bankers,[1] or *at-tujjār*, the merchants[2]; each of them is also referred to as *jahbadh al-Ahwāz*, the banker of the province of Ahwāz,[3] in which capacity they probably

of the Jewish population. Probably the appearance of Jewish bankers or government treasury officials in Baghdād was connected with the extraordinary financial needs of the State, which had to make use of the Jews in order to meet them. As to the treatise of al-Jāḥiẓ v. now also E. Fritsch, Islam und Christentum im Mittelalter (*Beiträge zur Geschichte der moslemischen Polemik gegen das Christentum in arabischer Sprache*), Breslau, 1930 ; he assigns the treatise of al-Jāḥiẓ to the reign of the Caliph al-Ma'mūn (813–833). *Vide* H. Hirschfeld, Mohammedan Criticism of the Bible, *JQR.*, xiii (1901), pp. 230–2, 239–240. Finkel characterizes this treatise as "unique in the whole range of Mohammedan polemical literature" (*JAOS.*, vol. xlvii (1927), pp. 312–328).

[4] Among the medical men named in our sources there are, judging by names and designations, apparently no Jews. *Vide Ibn al-Qifti*, pp. 104, 409 ; *Wuz.*, 244 ; H. Bowen, op. cit., pp. 184, 191, 327, 331–2 ; R. Levy, *A Baghdad Chronicle*, Cambridge, 1929, pp. 140–2. The influence of Christian secretaries and clerks must have been very powerful in the 'Abbāsid administration, in spite of the restrictive edict of al-Muqtadir. The sources note this fact with regret more than once. Christians were members of the most important Dīwāns. Cf. *Misk.*, 23, 143, 218 ; *'Arīb*, 30, 184. There was even a Christian army inspector and chairman of the Dīwān al-jaish.

[1] *'Arīb*, 74 ; *Wuz.*, 79–81 ; *Tan.*, ii, 81–5.

[2] *Wuz.*, 81 ; *Misk.*, 44, 66, 129 ; *Tan.*, ii, 85, 4–8.

[3] *Wuz.*, 81 ; *Tan.*, ii, 84 ; *Wuz.*, 178 ; جهبذ الاهواز

had to execute certain financial operations relating to the revenue from this province.

Besides these titles, which themselves indicate the important position they occupied in the financial administration of the 'Abbāsid empire, we find the names of Joseph b. Phineas and Aaron b. Amram also included in the extremely enlightening list of forms of address to the state and court officials of al-Muqtadir.[1] They are honoured there with the title "Court Bankers", *jahābidhat al-ḥaḍra* (جهابذة الحضرة), to whom a particular form of address was due. Undoubtedly these bankers were privileged Jews, whose relations with the Caliph and his Viziers were of the closest.

Nearly all the passages that tell us anything about dealings with Joseph b. Phineas and Aaron b. Amram represent them as acting conjointly. The state authorities, as we shall presently see, treat them as a unity, and when the Vizier is in need of money *both* are requested to appear at Court. The loan made to the Vizier is granted by contract conjointly with both Joseph b. Phineas and Aaron b. Amram, and the punishment with which the Vizier threatens them would have been borne by both Joseph b. Phineas and Aaron b. Amram.[2]

These indications suffice for us to infer that the two had formed themselves into a company, and to regard them as a single firm.[3] This firm may have included others besides Joseph b. Phineas and Aaron b. Amram. Such "others"

[1] *Wuz.*, 158–9. We suggest that وجهابذة be emended to وهم جهابذة. Besides these two Jews there was also a certain Zakariyyā b. Yūḥannā upon whom the honour of this title was conferred, but we do not hear anything of him or his activities elsewhere. L. Massignon (*La Passion d'al-Ḥallāj*, Paris, 1922, i, p. 266) thought that this Zakariyyā was also a Jew, but that is impossible. *Vide* now his *L'influence de l'Islam au moyen âge*, p. 5, n. 5, where he admits "peut-être un chrétien".

[2] See *Wuz.*, 80–1 ; *Tan.*, ii, 84–5.

[3] The Gaonic Responsa furnish abundant evidence of commercial partnerships and associated enterprises, etc., of this period. *Vide* J. Mann, *JQR.*, new series, x, 324. During the Middle Ages the formation of companies was also frequent among European Jews. *Vide* M. Hoffmann, *Der Geldhandel der deutschen Juden im Mittelalter*, Leipzig, 1910, p. 90.

are clearly alluded to in these expressions meaning "representatives" and "heirs".[1] Presumably they were sons or other relatives of the two principals. There is express mention of a son of Aaron b. Amram, who acted as *jahbadh* at court together with his father.[2]

The Vizier and the court generally must certainly have had a more or less concrete idea of those further partners of the banking firm, or else they would not have referred to them as they did.

The sources do not tell us for what reasons those court bankers had organized themselves so as to form a firm, but perhaps it was because of the considerable financial requirements to be met as *Hofjuden*, the fulfilment of which seems to have been beyond the capacity of a single individual; especially as at that time the risk of considerable financial operations was particularly great.[3] In any case, we have before us a single banking house, and in modern terminology it would probably have been appropriate to designate it as Joseph, Aaron and heirs, or Joseph, Aaron and Co., *Head Office, Baghdād.*[4]

We are not only able to describe the inner organization of that banking firm, but can also define more precisely the period of time during which these Jewish bankers were demonstrably connected with the Court.

First, we possess a direct testimony to the *terminus a quo* of their activity as court bankers,[5] namely that of at-Tanūkhi,

[1] *Wuz.*, 80; *Tan.*, ii, 84: ومن قام مقامهما and ورثتكما.

[2] *Misk.*, 128.

[3] There will be much to say regarding the internal management of this banking house further on, when its functions will be dealt with.

[4] In Baghdād there was a particular quarter where the money-changers and bankers were to be found. This "Wall Street" of Baghdād was called "'Aun-Street" درب العون. Cf. *Tan.*, i, p. 204; *Misk.*, 247–8; *Irshād*, i, 399; cf. *Islamic Culture*, 1931, p. 571. Would not our Court Jews have had their offices in this street? This street is not mentioned either in Le Strange, *Baghdad during the Abbasid Caliphate*, Oxford, 1900, or in M. Streck, *Die alte Landschaft Babylonien*, Leyden, 1900.

[5] This statement is only to be found so far in at-Tanūkhi's *Nishwār al-Muḥāḍara*, part ii, p. 84.

who says: "*The two (i.e. Joseph b. Phineas and Aaron b. Amram) were appointed in the time of 'Ubaidallah b. Yaḥyā al-Khāqāni.*" This statement, useful as it is, can, however, only accord with the other facts and dates given in the Arab sources if we regard the name 'Ubaidallah b. Yaḥyā as a textual error and read instead Muḥammad b. 'Ubaidallah b. Yaḥyā.

'Ubaidallah b. Yaḥyā [1] was Vizier under the Caliph al-Mutawakkil from 850 to 861 and under the Caliph al-Mu'tamid from 870 to 877. But the objection of those two sovereigns to the admission of *ahl adh-Dhimma* into the civil service is too well known to permit the assumption that Jews could have occupied high offices during their reigns; still less that Jews would have been appointed to high offices by them. Apart from its inherent improbability there is no evidence whatever in the sources to support such a supposition. On the other hand, Muḥammad b. 'Ubaidallah b. Yaḥyā, the son of 'Ubaidallah b. Yaḥyā, was one of al-Muqtadir's Viziers (912–913) and lived during the very period at which for the first time we find concrete data of these Jews and their activities. It is hardly possible to assume that they were active more than thirty years before any sources mention them; their appointment as court-bankers must rather have taken place when Muḥammad b. 'Ubaidallah was already Vizier, i.e. somewhere between 912 and 913. The facts agree with that; for the first financial transaction of these Jews mentioned in our sources took place in the year 908 and was carried out under the Vizier Ibn al-Furāt,[2] probably some years before the title of court-bankers, doubtless in recognition rather than in anticipation of services

[1] *Vide* E. de Zambaur, *Manuel de Généalogie et de Chronologie pour l'histoire de l'Islam*, Hannover, 1927, pp. 6, 7, 12; *Enc. Isl.*, ii, s.v.

[2] *Wuz.*, 80; *Tan.*, ii, 80. Regarding him, *vide Enc. Isl.*, ii, s.v. A monograph on this Vizier would be a valuable counterpart to the work of H. Bowen, on *'Ali b. 'Īsā*, and to that of H. Gottschalk, *Die Māḏarā'ijjūn*, Hamburg, 1931. *Vide* the short but excellent sketch of the Vizier Ibn al-Furāt by A. Mez, *Die Renaissance des Islam*, pp. 87–9.

rendered, was conferred upon them. During the following years we hear of them again and again, especially in 913,[1] 918,[2] 921,[3] 923,[4] 924,[5] which is a further confirmation of our hypothesis.

After their appointment they seem to have been in continuous contact with the court till 923. Perhaps the dismissal of the Vizier Ibn al-Furāt in 924–5, after his third term of office, accounts for the silence of the sources following 923 on the subject of this firm, whose patron and most important "client" he was. On the other hand, we are explicitly informed that "they were not dismissed until their deaths",[6] but the latter may have taken place about this time. In any case, al-Muqtadir's reign must be considered as the period in which these activities took place.

We may now attempt to determine the nature of these operations.

2. The Activities of the Jewish Bankers

If we describe as bankers those whose profession it is to administer, procure, and supply money,[7] we are indeed entitled to count Joseph b. Phineas and Aaron b. Amram

[1] *Tan.*, ii, 85; *Wuz.*, 81.

[2] *'Arīb*, 74.

[3] *Misk.*, 79. The privileged position of Aaron b. Amram at court can also be seen from the fact that he appears in the inner palace, as related in *Misk.*, 79 (reproduced in *'Arīb*, 91), in connection with the trial of al-Ḥallāj, as one of the usual visitors. Cf. the story of Ibn Zanji, apud L. Massignon, *Quatre textes inédits relatifs à la biographie d'al-Ḥallāj*, Paris, 1914, p. 9 L. Massignon, *La Passion d'al-Ḥallāj*, p. 266. From this passage it follows, indeed, that Aaron b. Amram was in charge of the state-prisoner al-Ḥallāj. Cf. L. Massignon, *L'influence*, etc., p. 3. Cf. *Misk.*, 128, where Aaron b. Amram and his son (الجهبذان) are to be found in the residence of the Vizier al-Khāqāni.

[4] *Misk.*, 112.

[5] *Misk.*, 128, where Aaron b. Amram appears together with his son.

[6] *Vide Tan.*, ii, 85. We shall see further on that after the death of the two principals their sons and grandsons took over the affairs. In the sources they are called "representatives" and "heirs".

[7] Max Weber, *Grundriss der Sozialökonomik II. Wirtschaft und Gesellschaft*, Tübingen, 1922, pp. 92–3.

as bankers in quite a modern sense; and, in view of their almost exclusive dealings with the Court and its officials, as Court Bankers in fact as well as in name.[1]

Their professional activities, to which we now turn, may be summed up under the following main categories:—

Financial Transactions.

(*a*) Administration of Funds.
(*b*) Remittance of Funds.
(*c*) Supply of Funds.

Mercantile Transactions.

(*a*) *Administration of Funds.*

The Arab sources of the tenth century reveal a prodigious desire to accumulate money, a mad rush to get rich. The appetite for money was only equalled by the fear of losing it.

This phenomenon will be discussed fully in another connection. Here it may suffice to state that officials and merchants, who were the mainstay of this money economy,[2] feared the interference of the State, which was easily able to gain possession of private property by the then almost universal method of confiscation (*muṣādara*).[3]

This feeling of fear and uncertainty caused people to look for the safest place in which to keep their money. To this end the oddest ways and methods were invented. Gold and silver were hidden under the soil,[4] in wells,[5] in cisterns,[6] in

[1] *Wuz.*, 158.

[2] *Vide* the sociologically instructive passage in *Tan.*, i, p. 243.

[3] As to the meaning of this word and the evolution of its significance, *vide* Cl. Huart, *ZDMG.*, vol. lxiii (1909), pp. 856–7, and A. Fischer, *ZDMG.*, vol. lxiv (1910), pp. 481–4.

[4] *Misk.*, 416; *Ecl.*, ii, 11–12, 74, 187. After the death of the Emīr Abū'l Ḥusain Bakhkam a list was made of all the places where his money was hidden.

[5] *Tan.*, ii, 210, tells us that more than 80,000 dīnārs were taken out of a well belonging to a merchant. Even the privy was used as a hiding-place for money; *vide* the detailed and amusing story in *Tan.*, i, 15–16. Other evidence in *Misk.*, 102, where the Vizier himself is said to have hidden no less than half a million dīnārs in cesspools. *Vide* also *Tan.*, i, 272.

[6] Ibn Sa'īd, ed. Tallquist, pp. 39–40.

barns,[1] among clothes, etc. Money was also invested in jewellery and trinkets, as well as other articles of luxury,[2] only in order to prevent the State from snatching away one's not always honestly gained wealth.[3] Owners of real estate could protect themselves against the danger of loss by constituting their landed property a Waqf,[4] whereby they at least could enjoy the revenue derived without fear. But what could be done with money hoards ? [5]

In addition to hiding their money in the ground and elsewhere, people began to deposit it with prominent persons,[6] merchants,[7] and above all with professional money-dealers or bankers. This method was used chiefly by the high officials themselves, and the Viziers of the Caliphs. The bankers and money-changers, whose profession it was to engage in money transactions, were for that very reason considered to be the proper, safe, and reliable people to entrust with one's fortune.[8]

So the habit was adopted by every Vizier of the age of

[1] *Misk.*, 230 ; this method is still in use in Algeria. Cf. on this A. Ruehl, *Vom Wirtschaftsgeist im Orient*, Leipzig, 1925, p. 42.

[2] at-Tanūkhi, *al-Faraj ba'd ash-Shidda*, i, 113 ; ii, 17. Cf. C. H. Becker, *Ägypten im Mittelalter, Islamstudien*, Leipzig, 1924, i, p. 183 : " Ausserdem war eine grosse Garderobe eine nicht zu verachtende Geldanlage in einer Zeit, der noch die Thesaurierung der Wertobjekte für sicherer galt als das Arbeitenlassen des Kapitals."

[3] Naturally immense fortunes simply disappeared, because after their owners' death nobody knew where their treasures were hidden ; and on the other hand great treasures were often discovered by mere chance. *Vide Misk.*, 299.

[4] For the Waqf as a measure against confiscation *vide* v. Kremer, *Einnahmebudget*, p. 16 ; Becker, *Beiträge*, pp. 266 ff., and *Islamstudien*, Leipzig, 1924, i, p. 62; also W. Bjoerkman, " Kapitalentstehung und = Anlage im Islam, Berlin," *MSOS.*, ii, 1930, pp. 80–98.

[5] When the chamberlain Naṣr heard that he was to be arrested he first of all hastened to deposit his money with others (*Misk.*, 117).

[6] *Vide Misk.*, 102, 68 ; *Irshād*, i, 70 ; v, 350 ; *Ecl.*, iii, 262.

[7] *Misk.*, 44 ; *Wuz.*, 74.

[8] That they were by no means absolutely safe is evident from *Misk.*, 257. al-Barīdi, the governor of Ahwāz, had the bankers' houses looted and took all the money that was found there, the bankers' own as well as that of their clients. As to مضارة cf. the lexica. Cf. also the story in Mubarrad, *Kāmil*, Cairo, 1308, i, 208.

al-Muqtadir to have his own money-keeper, his own particular banker.[1] Naturally care was taken not to have such deposits entered in books.[2] Thus Ibn al-Furāt is said to have deposited huge sums with merchants [3] and clerks without letting it be known.[4] Another official, for reasons of security, deposited a sum of 10,000 dīnārs with a banker without having it entered in either the debit or credit page of his books.[5] The important revenue-farmer, later Vizier, Ḥāmid b. ʿAbbās deposited with the banker Ibrāhīm b. Yuḥanna a sum of 100,000 gold dīnārs.[6] In the year 927, 10,000 dīnārs belonging to the Vizier al-Khasībi were found partly in strong boxes, partly in the custody of his *jahbadh.*[7]

It is only natural that our two Jewish bankers should also have been entrusted with such deposits. As court bankers they must have been considered particularly reliable and safe. Their clients were mostly high officials and Viziers, particularly the Vizier Ibn al-Furāt, of whose deposits with the Jewish banking firm we hear many other interesting things.

Thus Ibn al-Furāt, after his fall as Vizier, was finally forced to confess that he had deposited a sum of 160,000 dīnārs (consisting of *māl al-muṣādara*) with Aaron b. Amram and his son.[8] The Caliph al-Muqtadir summoned these two bankers, who confirmed the existence of this deposit and, at the Caliph's order, conveyed the money to his privy purse.[9]

We hear of other deposits of Ibn al-Furāt with the Jewish

[1] The banker of Ibn al-Furāt was Aaron b. Amram, as well as Joseph b. Phineas. Ibrāhīm b. Yūḥannā is said to have been the banker of Ḥāmid b. ʿAbbās (*Misk.*, 95 ; *Wuz.*, 226). ʿAli b. ʿĪsā also had his own ناقد named Ibn Abī ʿĪsā (*Wuz.*, 291 and 224). A جهبذ of the Vizier al-Khasībi is also mentioned in *Misk.*, 155.

[2] *Vide*, for instance, *Wuz.*, 79–80, and *Tan.*, ii, 83–5.

[3] These "merchants" mean the two Jewish court bankers, *vide* the section "Mercantile Transactions".

[4] *Misk.*, 44.

[5] *Tan.*, i, 103–4.

[6] *Misk.*, 95 ; *Wuz.*, 226.

[7] *Misk.*, 158. Here both methods of treasuring money had been used.

[8] *Misk.*, 128.

[9] *Wuz.*, 124. A parallel version in *Misk.*, 128, shows only slight variations.

bankers (الجهبذين اليهوديين) to which he had to confess in the course of the inquiry that was instituted against him. The Jews were obliged to convey the money to the public exchequer.[1]

Closely connected with their function of administering funds was the employment of this Jewish banking house as an address for certain illegal monies destined for the account of Ibn al-Furāt. Ibn al-Furāt was also the first to have funds (so-called "bribery money") [2] remitted directly to Aaron b. Amram,[3] who credited them to the former's account. The Vizier, of course, avoided creating any evidence of the existence of such an account in the form of book-keeping entries.[4]

We also learn [5] that this greedy Vizier had yet another money transaction with Aaron b. Amram and Joseph b. Phineas, which even led to a sort of legal inquiry against them. Here we are told in a very detailed manner how the Vizier increased his wealth by transmitting confiscated funds (*māl al-muṣādara*) not to the Caliph's privy purse or to the public exchequer as he should have done, but to his own secret account, which he had opened with the Jewish banking firm. To this passage

[1] *'Arīb*, 74, 13 ff.

[2] Cf. H. F. Amedroz, "Abbasid Administration in its Decay," *JRAS.*, 1913, pp. 834–5. *Māl al-marāfiq* was legitimate according to the financial morality of the time.

[3] *Wuz.*, 33.

[4] In view of the fact that the Hebrew characters were used in the bulk of Jewish-Arabic writings of the Middle Ages, including Gaonic literature, it might not be amiss to consider whether the account-books of these court bankers were kept in the Hebrew or in the Arabic script. Jewish court bankers of mediaeval Europe, we are told, kept their books not only in Hebrew script but sometimes in the Hebrew language, and then had them translated into Latin (cf. M. Hoffmann, *Der Geldhandel der deutschen Juden*, p. 117). There is an instance on record even from the sphere of modern Islam. Between the years 1825–7 Jews were engaged as bankers of the Pasha at Damascus. They had the monopoly of all government banking business. When they were dismissed as the result of intrigues their successors were unable to carry on the Pasha's business because their books had been kept in the Hebrew script. *Vide Revue de l'Académie Arabe à Damas*, 1922, pp. 600 ff.

[5] *Wuz.*, 78 ff.; *Tan.*, ii, 82 ff. The differences between the two versions of the text need not be taken into consideration here, as they do not affect the substance.

we owe not only further information on the bankers' function of administering funds,[1] but also a rather interesting insight into the way in which the *jahbadh* used to keep his accounts, and how these accounts were controlled by the Government.[2] For these bankers had to furnish a detailed report, and a statement of all the funds that had been entrusted to them, in connection with the inquiry carried out against the Vizier Ibn al-Furāt.[3]

(*b*) *Remittance of Funds.*

Our bankers not only took charge of deposits and administered funds but also transmitted money. We must remember that in those times the endorsement of bills was already coming into use. In the tenth century it was customary to pay debts not only in cash but also by means of letters of credit. For such letters of credit or cheques the expression *suftaja* (سفتجة) was used.[4] The purpose of this *suftaja* was to convey money from place to place without incurring the risk of transport.[5] It was thus a means of avoiding payments in coin to distant places. By means of such a *suftaja*, whose very essence is transaction at a distance,[6] the tradesman was able to carry larger amounts

[1] This passage, too, gives us an idea of the very considerable sums that passed through their hands.

[2] The control of the books of the *jahbadh* by the government apparently implies the official character of this office.

[3] The text uses the expression ختمات for these reports. We find the same expression in connection with the activities of a *jahbadh* in *Misk.*, 155, 158, 164–6. It shows that these *khatamāt* were kept in the Vizier's Dīwān. Cf. *Kitāb Mafātiḥ al-ʿUlūm*, p. 54. *Vide* also *Tan.*, i, 42, 109, 176. The *jahbadh* had to write detailed receipts (روز) for all money matters.

[4] The economic and legal nature of the *suftaja* is the object of detailed explanations by the Arab lexicographers. Wahrmund, *Handwörterbuch*, s.v., renders the expression with " Kreditbrief ". Belot, *Vocab.*, with " lettre de change " ; Amedroz (*Gloss.*, p. 62) with " bill of exchange ".

[5] For the whole question see R. Grasshoff, *Die suftaǧa und ḥawāla der Araber*, Göttingen, 1899, pp. 1–36.

[6] According to L. Goldschmidt, *Universalgeschichte des Handelsrechts*, Stuttgart, 1891, pp. 403–4, the essence of a bill transaction is the real or ideal movement of sums of money. According to the conception of mediaeval law a difference of place between remitter and remittee is indispensable to a bill of change.

with him, or to convey them without incurring the risks which, in the case of cash, were considerable in those days.[1] Thus we hear that a man made a long journey with only two servants and a guide, while his earthly riches consisted of *suftajas* for 5,000 dīnārs.[2]

Money presents were brought from the Ahwāz province to the Caliph's mother in the form of a *suftaja* for the amount of 3,000 dīnārs.[3] Even bribes were paid in this way.[4]

The new Arab sources show very clearly a widespread use of that safe and easy method of payment,[5] which simplified the manifold mercantile relations of the 'Abbāsid empire of those times and was very useful for the rapid and safe settlement of business matters.[6]

The contemporary Jewish sources, too, i.e. the Gaonic Responsa, throw light on the functions and scope of the *suftaja*.[7]

For instance, the money for the Babylonian academies was conveyed from Kairuwān [8] to Sura or Pumbadita by means of such letters of credit, and it can be assumed that other far-off communities employed the same method.[9]

[1] *Vide Misk.*, 219, where a ship (شذاة, cf. Lane, *Dict.*, s.v.) carrying the revenues of Ahwāz to Baghdād is robbed (year 319/931).

[2] *Tan.*, i, 104, 5.

[3] *Tan.*, i, 105.

[4] *Tan.*, i, 103. Further proofs in our texts : *Tan.*, i, 90, 93 ; ii, 680, etc. ; *Wuz.*, 93 ff.

[5] We learn the same from Arab papyrus fragments ; cf. H. C. Becker, *Papyri Schott-Reinhard*, Heidelberg, 1906, i, p. 11.

[6] R. Grasshoff's opinion, loc. cit., 10, "Ganz versagen für die Erforschung der inneren Beschaffenheit des arabischen Handels und damit für die Erkenntnis der Funktionen der suftağa die Historiker des Islams," is therefore now out of date.

[7] Cf. A. Harkavy, *Tshuboth ha-Geonim : Studien und Mitteilungen*, Berlin, 1887, iv, No. 423 (pp. 216, 316), No. 548 (p. 209), No. 552 (pp. 273–4). All responsa dealing with *suftaja* are written in Arabic and not in Hebrew. Harkavy renders the word *suftaja* by "Wechselschein" or "Anweisung", p. 316, No. 6.

[8] Cf. now also J. Mann, *Texts and Studies in Jewish History and Literature*, Cincinnati, i, 1931, pp. 143–4.

[9] On *suftaja* from Basra to Baghdād, v. Harkavy, ibid., Nos. 548, 552. On later conditions of trade and cheques in Basra, cf. the evidence of Nāṣir-i Khosrau, ed. Schefer, p. 64. Cf. Mez, ibid., 447 ff.

This *suftaja*-system was a source of legal problems for the Jewish authorities; as, for instance, the question whether, according to Talmudic civil law, a legal claim was tenable should such a letter of credit be lost. The Gaon's answer was that the principles of Talmudic civil law did not admit the legality of a claim in case of loss. But as the Beth Dīn saw that such letters of credit continued to be used, it finally took up such claims in order not to hinder the commercial relations among merchants.[1]

This *suftaja*-system not only furthered private commerce and communication[2] but also helped to simplify and rationalize the financial administration of the government. For now these letters of credit were also used as a means of sending the taxes from the provinces of the ʿAbbāsid empire to the public exchequer in Baghdād.[3] Our sources tell us that in 916 the public exchequer in Baghdād contained *amwāl safātij* that had come from Fārs, Iṣfahān, and the Eastern provinces.[4] ʿAli b. ʿĪsā, who was then the financial inspector of Egypt and Syria, had 147,000 dīnārs of taxes sent by his chamberlain from Egypt to Baghdād by means of *suftaja*.[5]

The revenue farmers of Ahwāz,[4] of Iṣfahān,[4] and Fārs also made use of this *suftaja*-system, and chose this way of sending their money to the public exchequer. It seems that there were special messengers (فيج), whose task it was to carry the letters with the *suftaja* to Baghdād.[6]

[1] Harkavy, ibid., No. 423, apud J. Mann in *JQR.*, x, p. 324. For the illegality of the *suftaja* according to Islamic theory, cf. Th. W. Juynboll, *Handbuch d. islamischen Gesetzes*, 1910, p. 274. It was regarded as a kind of loan which resulted in an illicit benefit to the parties.

[2] A typical piece of evidence for the flourishing state of commerce and the commonness of letters of credit, etc., is *Ecl.*, iii, pp. 138–9, towards the end of the tenth century. "What a marvellous sight to see a bill of change (خط) on a commercial enterprise drawn in the enemy's country! If this is a source of pride, then the merchants are more powerful than the Viziers in East and West, for the former draw bills on high amounts . . . that are accepted with more readiness than tribute and land-tax."

[3] *Misk.*, 43.

[4] *Misk.*, 187.

[5] *Wuz.*, 296; *Misk.*, 146; v. also *Ibn Saʿīd*, ed. Tallquist, p. 32.

[6] *Misk.*, 150.

In any case, this system of payment seems to have been so common and familiar also in the accounting offices of the treasury department that the author of the work *Mafātīḥ al-'Ulūm*, in explaining the 'Abbāsid administrative terminology, has nothing to say of the word *suftaja* but معروف " is well known ".[1]

These letters of credit, which were sent to the public exchequer from various eastern and western provinces of the 'Abbāsid empire, had, of course, to be cashed and exchanged. It happened not unfrequently that *safātij* were left uncashed in the public exchequer or in the Vizier's archives, and were simply forgotten because of the responsible official's negligence. The Arab sources mention several cases of such muddled management in the exchequer.[2]

Nevertheless it may be assumed that they were cashed in most cases. Our texts do not tell us very much about the methods of cashing, neither do we learn how the governmental accounting offices dealt with the *suftaja* in their accounts. But it can hardly be doubted that the settlement of *suftaja* business was connected primarily with those officials who were employed as *jahbadh*. This may be inferred from the case of the kindred institution of *ṣakk* (صكّ).[3]

The bankers were the natural money-changers and agents in such payments, and must have played an important part whenever such letters of credit were exchanged. Among others, our sources mention transactions of that kind by the Jewish bankers. In reading the following lines we get the impression of a modern money order [4] :—

[1] Ed. v. Vloten, p. 62. [2] Cf. *Misk.*, 23 ; 262, 2 ; 350.

[3] Cf. primarily *Irshād*, vol. i, 385, 399; also *Wuz.*, 73, 77, 235; *Misk.*, 158, 6; ii, 80 (صكّ على الجهبذ) ; Ibn Hauqal, pp. 42, 70 ; *Tan.*, i, 109 ; *Ecl.*, iii, 46 ff., 119. *Vide* G. Jacob, " Die ältesten Spuren des Wechsels," *MSOS.*, 1925, pp. 280–1 ; *Mafātīḥ al-'Ulūm*, pp. 56–7. Cf. Dīwān of Ibn al-Mu'tazz (*ZDMG.*, xl, p. 581). On an occurrence of the verb صكّ as early as the first century A.H. in connection with ذكر حق cf. Balādhuri, *Ansāb al-Ashrāf*, v, p. 58, ed. S. D. Goitein, Jerusalem, 1936.

[4] *Misk.*, 112. A parallel version in *Wuz.*, 306–7.

"The Vizier Ibn al-Furāt then took his ink-pot and wrote an order to his banker (*jahbadh*) Aaron b. Amram, telling him to pay from his account and without further notice 2,000 dīnārs to ʻAli b. ʻĪsā, as a subvention towards the payment of a fine imposed upon him. Muḥassin b. al-Furāt also ordered his banker to pay this ʻAli b. ʻĪsā 1,000 dīnārs from his account that was in Aaron b. Amram's bank." [1]

This money conveyance business, conducted in cash as well as by means of *suftajas*, must also have been a source of income to the bankers, and it may be supposed that they got a certain commission for cashing *suftaja*, as we know them to have got one for cashing *ṣakk*.[2] The relationship between our court bankers and the *suftaja* system can also be inferred from the fact that the Vizier deposited unpaid *suftajas* with the Jewish bankers Joseph b. Phineas and Aaron b. Amram as security for a considerable loan that the Vizier desired to obtain from them. But this leads us to another, the most important, of their business activities.

(c) *Supply of Funds.*

As the money requirements of the Caliph and the State became more and more considerable, the rapid supply of funds, especially for military purposes, became urgently necessary.

These extraordinary money needs gave birth to various methods of money supply. The method of revenue farming, of indirect levying of taxes, was already employed as a way of overcoming financial difficulties. The revenue farmer had to pay the Caliph a certain fixed lump sum, and moreover he undertook to pay the State partly in advance, thus enabling it to obtain cash quickly. But other methods were

[1] The newly appointed Vizier thus helps the fallen Vizier to bear his fine, which is rather a strange practice. It was probably the result of the Vizier's realization that the same fate might very soon be his own. Cf. C. H. Becker, *Islamstudien*, i, p. 205.

[2] The usual rate seems to have been one dirham per dīnār.

also used against financial crises. New departments and offices were created, the administration was divided and subdivided into numberless offices and functions, not from administrative but from purely financial motives, i.e. in order to increase the revenue of the State by selling such posts. The selling of offices to the highest bidder was a frequent occurrence, as was also the sale of crown lands and the arbitrary confiscation of private fortunes. The Caliph's privy purse was squeezed to the last farthing, so that it could no longer be considered a reserve fund against emergencies. The Viziers, the responsible chancellors of the empire's exchequer, could hardly find any way out; for even the systematic economies of 'Ali b. 'Īsā, who reduced salaries, pensions, and other expenses, were not able to balance the budget.

It was probably in this situation that the idea occurred to the Caliph of calling in the aid of the Jewish bankers in consolidating the finances of the State. It is permissible to infer from the picture the sources present of Aaron b. Amram and Joseph b. Phineas, that their importance for the financial economy of al-Muqtadir's empire lay in their capacity of money-suppliers and money-lenders. This was really the centre of gravity of their business activity, far surpassing in significance all the other financial activities discussed above.

We are able to reconstruct, with the help of our Arab sources, their functions as money-suppliers in many details.

We know of three instances of credits being extended to the State by these financiers.

(1) In *Wuz.*, 178, we hear that the Vizier Ibn al-Furāt, during his first vizierate,[1] called the Jewish banker (*al-jahbadh al-yahūdī*) Joseph b. Phineas,[2] who is designated as جهبذ الاهواز, and asked him for an advance of money in order to pay salaries for the officials of Ahwāz for two months (*māl shahrain*). It was indicated that as official tax-collector of

[1] Probably about the year 311/923.

[2] The text reads يوسف بن فيجاس.

the province of Ahwāz he had sufficient guarantees in the form of later taxes.[1] But Joseph b. Phineas was not so readily induced to grant the loan. Nevertheless, as the report continues, Ibn al-Furāt did not stop arguing with him until he finally assented and on the very same day granted a loan for a month. Of course, Ibn al-Furāt without delay ordered his servant to fetch the amount from Joseph b. Phineas.

(2) The Vizier ʿAli b. ʿĪsā, too, was obliged to ask the Jewish bankers for a loan in order to consolidate the public budget. He addressed them as follows[2]:—

"Do you want to avoid my inflicting penalties on you[3] that may affect you and your heirs (عليكما وعلى ورثتكما) for ever? I shall only refrain from it in consideration of a matter that will cause you no damage whatever. At the beginning of each month I need an amount of 30,000 dīnārs, which must be paid within the first six days to the infantry troops.[4] However, I am usually not in possession of such a sum, neither on the first nor on the second day of the month. I want you, therefore, to advance on the first of each month a loan of 150,000 dirhams, an amount that you, as you know, will get back in the course of the month from the Ahwāz revenue. For the administration of the Ahwāz revenue belongs to you (جهبذة الاهواز اليكما), and these moneys (from

[1] Only Joseph b. Phineas is mentioned here as جهبذ الاهواز. Cf., however, *Wuz.*, 81, and *Tan.*, ii, 84–5, where both Joseph b. Phineas and Aaron b. Amram are referred to as connected with جهبذة الاهواز.

[2] This and the following passage occurs in two versions, but they do not show any important changes (*Wuz.*, 80–1; *Tan.*, ii, 84–5).

[3] The Vizier merely used this threat in order to force the Jewish bankers to comply with his aim. For they were not culpable, as is evident from the whole course of events.

[4] Loans were usually occasioned by urgent expenditure for military purposes. That it was military expenditure that rendered a loan necessary is not accidental. The need of capital for army purposes weighed most heavily on the budget. So that it was precisely in the financing of the army that the credit system developed entirely new methods. The influence of the troops, mostly Turkish mercenaries, on the administration as a whole kept steadily increasing.

Ahwāz) are a permanent advance of money to you, to which I am going to add (as security) the amount of 20,000 dīnārs that are payable every month by Ḥāmid b. ʿAbbās.[1] This will be the compensation for the first instalment [and I shall be relieved of a heavy burden]." [2]

The two bankers, so we hear, made difficulties at first and intended to refuse,[3] but the Vizier did not stop urging them until they gave their consent.

(3) In his request to this banking firm to give him a loan, the Vizier ʿAli b. ʿĪsā could offer the future revenue from the province of Ahwāz and other sources of income as securities and guarantees. But we also hear of another application for a loan by this Vizier—probably during his first vizierate, in the year 913—to the same banking firm, in which a fiscal method appears that had probably not been used by anyone before in the course of ʿAbbāsid financial policy.

"When the Vizier ʿAli b. ʿĪsā had to make payments for which he had no funds, he would take from the merchants [4] a loan (استسلف) of 10,000 dīnārs, the security for which consisted of letters of credit (*suftaja*) which had come in from the provinces but were not yet due, and by giving interest at the rate of $1\frac{1}{2}$ silver dānaqs on the dīnār, which made the amount of 2,500 dirhams a month. This arrangement was made with Joseph b. Phineas and Aaron b. Amram and their representatives (ومن قام مقامهما) for the period of sixteen years [and after their death]." [5]

In this agreement we have no less than the taking of a well-covered long-term loan by the government from the

[1] Here the *muṣādara* of this dismissed Vizier is referred to.

[2] The words in brackets are only to be found in at-Tanūkhi.

[3] The difficulties at first made by the two bankers here show that they did not have much faith at that time in the solvency of the State. The refusal of merchants or bankers to give money to the State often led, however, to acts of violence. Cf. for a later instance, *Ecl.*, iii, p. 282.

[4] With the name of "merchants" the two Jewish bankers and their firm were designated.

[5] *Wuz.*, 81, 8–13 ; *Tan.*, ii, 85, 4–8. Cf. v. Kremer, *Einnahmebudget*, p. 14.

Jewish bankers, that was carried out with all the elements of an almost modern banking technique. And this more than a full millennium ago! Without going into details about this document, attention must be called to some particulars that are of importance for the history of finance generally, namely:—

(*a*) The negotiation of a state loan as such.[1]

(*b*) The payment of interest.[2]

(*c*) The pledging of uncashed letters of credit as security.

(*d*) The state's entering into an agreement with a Jewish banking house.

Mercantile Transactions

In reviewing the financial transactions of these court bankers as represented by our authorities, one must ask: How were they enabled to meet the very considerable money requirements of the State? For even if we admit that the guarantees and securities they received, as, for instance, the

[1] The method of avoiding a financial crisis by taking up a loan seems to have become usual only at this period. A history of government loans in 'Abbāsid times, which ought to be written, would comprise all the methods of raising money على سبيل القرض (cf. *Misk.*, 164, 213, 220; *Ecl.*, iii, 159, 259 ff.). This method was also employed later on in the reign of the Caliph ar-Rāḍī by the Vizier Ibn Muqla (on this Vizier, v. the study of A. H. Harley in *Bulletin of the School of Oriental Studies*, London, 1923–5, iii, pp. 213 ff.), who obtained a loan (قرض) from the merchants, but was not able to pay it back, so that he had to give them bills on certain revenues and sell them crown lands (*Misk.*, 329; cf. *Misk.*, 299). This is the origin of Islâmic feudalism, as will be shown elsewhere. For loans in the Egypt of that period, cf. C. H. Becker, *Beiträge zur Geschichte Aegyptens unter dem Islam*, Strassburg, 1900, pp. 38–9, 56; Mez, ibid., 123, 450.

[2] 'Ali b. 'Īsā was probably the first to obtain a loan by paying interest. Cf. v. Kremer, *Einnahmebudget*, pp. 7, 24, 63. The usual interest rate was a dirham for each dīnār, at which rate Abū Bekr b. Qarāba granted a loan to the Vizier (*Misk.*, 213, 220). According to *Tan.*, i, 204, a money-changer charges a commission rate of 1 dirham per dīnār. On the relation between dirham and dīnār cf. K. W. Hofmeyer, *Beiträge zur arabischen Papyrusforschung, Islam*, iv, 1913, pp. 100 ff.; further instances in the books of the Arab geographers; cf. also *Misk.*, 398, 3; 417, 5.

revenues of Ahwāz, were cashed in due course, we must still wonder whence they derived such immense money reserves of liquid cash. What, then, were the sources of their wealth ?

Their various kinds of business, such as administration, remittance, and supplying of funds, must certainly be considered a more or less important source of profit.[1] We may suppose that, first and foremost, the amounts deposited with them by court officials and Viziers (as we have seen, they were no small sums) [2] were not only hoarded, i.e. kept in the strict sense of the word. In all probability they were made productive, i.e. utilized as "capital" that "worked" for them.[3]

We must, however, take another source of their wealth into consideration ; namely, the trade in goods carried on by these "bankers". It must be remembered here that Joseph b. Phineas and Aaron b. Amram are also called expressly "the merchants" (*at-tujjār*).[4] Our sources often use this expression when they mean our *jahābidha*. It can hardly

[1] It is a matter of controversy whence the Jewish capitalists of mediaeval Europe derived their fortunes. Cf. for the various theories on this, accumulated ground-rent, profit on landed property or commercial undertakings, the work of M. Hoffmann, *Der Geldhandel der deutschen Juden*, Leipzig, 1910, and W. Sombart, *Die Juden und d. Wirtschaftsleben*, Leipzig, 1911.

[2] The sums of deposits only given by the Vizier Ibn al-Furāt amounted to millions of dīnārs. Cf. *Tan.*, ii, 82–4 ; *Wuz.*, 79–80, etc.

[3] Thus at a time when the unproductive treasuring of precious metals was widespread, certain circles were already using money otherwise than as a means of storing wealth.

[4] *Wuz.*, 81 ; *Tan.*, ii, 85. In the work of Miskawaih the name of Joseph b. Phineas does not appear at all. *Misk.* also avoids the expression *al-jahbadhān al-yahūdiyyān* in contrast to *Wuz.*, *Tan.*, and *'Arīb*. He refers to the two bankers with the more general denomination *at-tujjār*. There is no doubt, for instance, that by this word *Misk.*, 44, 66, and other passages can only mean our two bankers. This is clearly proved by a parallel version in *'Arīb*, 74, where the same fact is related with the identical details, except that جهبذ is used instead of تاجر. We have, therefore, reason for considering the words عند جماعة من التجار in *Misk.*, 44 (the Vizier Ibn al-Furāt had deposited considerable sums there), as well as the words in *Misk.*, 129, to refer to the Jewish banking firm with which the Vizier, as we saw above, used to deposit large amounts of money.

be supposed that the authors of our texts, high administrative officials whose profession developed the ability to distinguish sharply between departments, denominations, and titles, should simply have used the expression "*at-tujjār*" instead of *al-jahābidha* for no reason. It is improbable that this is merely a case of terminological looseness; on the contrary, we are bound to infer from this difference in expression that these Jews actually dealt in merchandise as well, although it is only their financial dealings that the Arab sources show in all their variety and many-sidedness. However, our assumption that they were engaged in mercantile transactions is not based on terminological evidence alone but is also justified by historical evidence. Business in money and business in goods were closely connected throughout the Middle Ages.[1] Money-lending is only an evolution of trade, and the economic history of the Middle Ages furnishes many instances of the fact that finance originates in commerce. The latter created the capital for money dealings of large scope. This process was also deeply rooted in the economic structure of the epoch in which these Court-Jews lived and worked. They probably began as merchants in the proper sense of the word, prospered, and finally turned to money affairs on a large scale. Their firm, presumably a trading house at first, thus developed into a banking firm, and their purely financial undertakings gradually pushed all their other commercial activities into the background.[2]

[1] In the Middle Ages financial affairs were conducted by merchants. The founder of the Rothschild banking firm, too, was at first a wholesale trader. Cf. R. Ehrenberg, *Das Zeitalter der Fugger*, i, Jena, 1922. J. Kulischer, *Warenhändler und Geldausleiher im Mittelalter*, p. 254, says: "Warenhandel und Geldhandel der verschiedensten Art, insbesondere das verzinsliche Darlehensgeschäft, sind im Mittelalter aufs engste miteinander verbunden. Der Kaufmann, der mit Waren handelt, ist zu gleicher Zeit auch Geldhändler, insbesondere Geldausleiher und umgekehrt." Note Sombart's saying (op. cit., p. 222): "Aus der Geldleihe ist der Kapitalismus geboren."

[2] Their trade probably comprised the same articles of Oriental commerce as are mentioned in the report on the "Rādānites". *Vide* J. Mann, *JQR.*, x, p. 330.

The Sources of their Financial Capacity

That these Jewish bankers in their capacity of money suppliers, however, were not dependent only on their own capital, on the amounts deposited with them, and on the profits derived from their mercantile activities, can be seen from a passage in at-Tanūkhi's *Nishwār al-Muḥāḍara* (second volume), and only there. In connection with the loan agreement made with 'Ali b. 'Īsā we read the following most enlightening statement about these bankers :—

" *For they were never dismissed until their death ; and they were appointed in the days of 'Ubaidallah b. Yaḥyā al-Khāqāni.*[1] *The Caliph did not want to dismiss them, in order to uphold the dignity of the office of* jahbadh *in the eyes of the merchants, so that the merchants might be ready to lend their money through the* jahbadh *if necessary. Were a* jahbadh *to be dismissed and another appointed in his place with whom the merchants had not yet had any dealings, the business of the Caliph would come to a standstill.*" [2]

That it was possible to speak of Jewish bankers in such a way is itself sufficient to show how much they were honoured and trusted by the Caliph, and, what is more important still, how indispensable they seem to have been to the Court. The part they played must really have been a very considerable one, for though the Caliph, in the twenty-five years of his reign, changed his Vizier no less than fifteen times, and though during that period the whole administrative machinery was subject to constant changes and the general situation was less stable than it had ever been, he did not want to dismiss these Jewish bankers but kept them in office for life.[3]

[1] *Vide* my above suggested emendation of this statement.

[2] This statement is to be found only *Tan.*, ii, ed. Margoliouth, Damascus, 1930, p. 85.

[3] *Wuz.*, 224–7, furnishes a detailed list containing the names of all the high officials and personalities who were condemned to pay a fine (*muṣādara*), including names of Viziers, governors, Dīwān heads, revenue farmers, etc. It is significant that Joseph b. Phineas and Aaron b. Amram are not

But to this passage we owe more than this evidence alone. We could hardly have hoped for a more enlightening answer as to the *sources of their financial capacity*, their activity as creditors, and the nature of their banking business generally. For we now see that as sources of capital they could rely not only on their own fortune or the deposits they administered, but also on the credit and confidence of other rich merchants of their time. The secret of their privileged position at Court is to be explained by their apparently unique ability, in virtue of their office, their reputation, the esteem and trust they commanded, as well as their manifold connections with commercial circles, to secure from the merchants the sums of liquid money necessary for meeting the requirements of the State and the Court.

What concrete details may we infer as to these "merchants", the *jahābidha's* connection with whom the Government valued so highly? The commercial activities of that time were not limited to any particular section of the population, so that, *a priori*, non-Jews are by no means excluded. Everybody was caught by the tidal wave of commercial prosperity with its chances of gain. Christians as well as Jews were bankers (جهبذ), money-changers (صيرفي), and merchants (تاجر), and so were, especially as regards the two last-mentioned classes, Muslims.[1]

Nevertheless, it is probably co-religionists of Joseph b. Phineas and Aaron b. Amram that are primarily meant. This view is not a little supported by the reference in our passage to the feelings of solidarity and personal confidence which unite those "merchants" with the two court bankers.

mentioned, though the black list contains several persons that bore the title of *jahbadh*. This, too, can be used as an argument in favour of their privileged position at Court.

[1] That Mohammedans, despite the Qur'ānic prohibition, apparently engaged in money-lending and in a considerable amount of speculation, particularly in crops, can be proved from numerous instances. Mohammedans as money-changers are mentioned i.a. in '*Arīb*, 135; *Tan.*, i, 272; *Ecl.*, ii, 307, and in many other passages.

It was just for this psychologically important reason that the Caliph never dismissed them. For only by keeping them in office, as the text informs us, could he "uphold the dignity of their office" in the merchants' eyes and borrow money through them.

The factor of solidarity, which economic historians have long recognized as a characteristic feature of Jewish participation in economic life,[1] was here, too, a factor of outstanding importance. In the tenth century this Jewish solidarity was especially well developed because of the peculiar cultural and religious organization of mediaeval Jewry. We know that at this period, known in Jewish history as the Gaonic era, Babylonian Jewry was in active contact with all parts of the Jewish Diaspora (Khorasān, Persia, Palestine, Egypt, North Africa, Spain, etc.). This close connection was due to the position of the Babylonian academies of Sura and Pumbadita, which were regarded by all those Jewish communities as their religious centre. These relations took the form not only of voluminous correspondence on questions of religious law between communities desirous of guidance and the spiritual head, the Gaon, but also of money contributions from abroad for the upkeep of these academies.[2] This cultural and religious hegemony of Babylonian Jewry was partly the cause and partly the result of an economic hegemony parallel to the general economic

[1] M. Hoffmann, *Der Geldhandel der deutschen Juden im Mittelalter*, p. 7; W. Roscher, *Die Stellung der Juden im Mittelalter*, p. 506; Kiesselbach, *Der Gang des Welthandels im Mittelalter*, p. 45; Franz Oppenheimer, *System der Soziologie*, vol. iv, Jena, 1935; Caro, *Sozial- und Wirtschaftsgeschichte der Juden im Mittelalter*, Leipzig, 1908; W. Sombart, *Die Juden u. d. Wirtschaftsleben*, pp. 200 ff. J. Mann, *JQR.*, x, n.s., p. 325, justly remarks: Of great furtherance for the expansion of the Jewish trade must have been the solidarity that existed among Jews all over the Diaspora." The Hebrew language also seems to have played an important unifying part herein.

[2] "The Jews of all countries contributed generously and freely to the upkeep of the seats of learning in Babylon and in Palestine" (Mann, *JQR.*, x, p. 39).

and political supremacy of Baghdād as capital of the 'Abbāsid Caliphate.

The merchants connected with our court Jews very probably included not only residents of Baghdād or Babylonia but also persons living in the more remote provinces of the Islamic empire. Relations with *Egypt* evidently existed.

Egypt and Babylonia were closely connected in those times, spiritually as well as economically. "Egyptian Jewry," says Mann, "no doubt received spiritual guidance from the Babylonian Gaons and their academies . . . on the other hand, the Babylonian schools in their turn obtained a good deal of material support, especially from the numerous Babylonian co-religionists that resided in Egypt." [1]

That relations with the province of *Ahwāz* must have existed is evident not only from the fact that Joseph b. Phineas and Aaron b. Amram were called the bankers of that province (جهبذ الاهواز) [2] but also from the circumstance that this province was the stronghold of commercial, and Jewish commercial, activity.[3] In the ninth century Ahwāz was already a station and a commercial "*point d'appui*" for the Jewish merchants known as the "Rādānites".[4] In its

[1] *JQR.*, x, loc. cit.

[2] *Vide Wuz.*, 81, 178; *Tan.*, ii, 84.

[3] Ahwāz was one of the most lucrative provinces of the 'Abbāsid Empire; cf. *Misk.*, 335, where it is said: "When the revenue of Ahwāz will stop, the empire will cease to exist." Cf. also *Misk.*, 349–350.

[4] Ibn Khordādhbeh, p. 153; Ibn al-Fakīh, p. 270. There is already a considerable literature on the Rādānites. However, no satisfactory explanation of the name has yet been given. One of the recent conjectures is that of Simonsen, who considers them to have been traders from the Rhone valley, i.e. "Rhodanici": "Il ne me parait pas invraisemblable que les Radanites . . . sont des 'Rhodanici' c'est à dire des marchands et des navigateurs du pays du Rhone," *REJ.*, 1907 (54), pp. 141–2. *Vide*—to cite a few names taken from the literature on the subject—J. Schipper, *Der Anteil der Juden am europäischen Grosshandel mit dem Orient in "Heimkehr"*, ed. v. Kellner, 1912, pp. 138–172; Scheffer-Boichorst, *Zur Geschichte der Syrer im Abendlande: Mitteilungen des Institutes für oesterreichische Geschichtsforschung*, vi, p. 544; de Goeje, *Internationaal Handelsverkeer in de Middeleeuwen, Opuscula*, iv, Amsterdam, 1908;

principal towns lived large Jewish communities which occupied an important economic position. The greater part of the merchants of Tustar,[1] we are explicitly told, were Jews. In Iṣfahān, whose economic importance won for it the title of " the second Baghdād ", the so-called Yahūdiyya [2] quarter had long been known as a great centre of trade and commerce. In Ahwāz [3] city, whose economic leadership is celebrated by all the Arab geographers, the Arab sources mention, no doubt by reason of their prominent position, a Jewish money-changer named Ya'qūb,[4] an Isrā'īl b. Ṣāliḥ,[5] and a Sahl b. Naẓīr [6] as the bankers (*jahbadh*) of the Governor al-Barīdi. Sīrāf,[7] in the tenth century a world-port and a clearing-house for trade between the Yemen, Persia, and China, then had a Jewish Governor (عامل) by the name of Rūzbah (Rozbih), the Persian equivalent of the Hebrew " Yom-tob ".[8]

These few data alone justify the inference of widespread international Jewish economic activity in the province of Ahwāz and other parts of the 'Abbāsid empire, and it is at

W. Heyd, *Histoire du commerce du Levant*, Leipzig, 1923, i, pp. 125 ff. Whether any relations existed between these Jewish merchants of the ninth century coming from the West and the predecessors of our banking firm of the tenth century cannot be elicited from the sources.

[1] *Misk.*, 257. The Jewish business men of Tustar are regarded as bankers, not as manufacturers ; cf. also W. Heyd, *Histoire du commerce du Levant*, Leipzig, 1923, i, pp. 29 f., 34 f. The " Banū Sahl ", the celebrated bankers and merchants of Egypt at the court of aẓ-Ẓāhir and al-Mustanṣir in the eleventh century, were originally of Tustar. See special chapter.

[2] *Muqadd.*, 388, 400 ; *Ibn al-Fakīh*, 254, 267 ; *Iṣṭakhri*, 182, 199. See also W. Fischel : *Yahūdiyya : On the beginning of the Jewish Settlement in Persia*, Tarbiz (Hebrew), Jerusalem, 1935, vol. vi, pp. 523 ff.

[3] Cf. P. Schwarz, *Iran im Mittelalter nach den arabischen Geographen*, Leipzig, 1896 ff., v. Index. The existence of Jewish merchants in Ahwāz is also attested by a Jewish-Persian document of the year 1020 ; see W. Fischel in *Enc. Jud.*, vol. ix, s.v. *Jüdisch-Persisch*, pp. 557 ff. Cf. D. S. Margoliouth, *JQR.*, xi, pp. 671–5.

[4] *Misk.*, 350.

[5] *Misk.*, 349 ; *Ecl.*, ii, 52.

[6] *Misk.*, 349, 379. About a Sahl b. Naẓīr of the third century cf. *Tan.*, *in Islamic Culture*, 1930, p. 181.

[7] *Ecl.*, ii, 218, 301.

[8] *Ecl.*, iii, 149–150.

least not unreasonable to seek here some of the " merchants " upon whom the court bankers drew for funds to finance the administration of the State.[1]

In any case, the material we have presented shows clearly that a commercial and banking organization was in existence at the beginning of the tenth century ; its centre lay in Baghdād, its heads were Joseph b. Phineas and Aaron b. Amram, the two Jews who acted as court bankers, and who had close business connections with rich merchants, Jews or non-Jews, of Baghdād, Ahwāz, and other parts of the Islamic empire. All these fulfilled an important function in the economic life of the 'Abbāsid Caliphate, and by repeatedly supplying the money needs of the State, helped to stave off its ruin.

[1] That the Jews of Baghdād and Babylonia continued to engage in financial operations at a later period is attested by other sources. I only wish to point out some cases here : in the MS. al-Hamadhāni, Takmilat Ta'rīkh aṭ-Ṭabari, Paris No. 1469, a Jewish banker Aaron is mentioned under the year 941 as the *jahbadh* of Ibn Shīrzād (هارون اليهودى جهبذ ابن شيرزاد). He is probably the one who is frequently mentioned in the newly published work of aṣ-Ṣūli, *Akhbār ar-Rāḍī wal-Muttaqī*, ed. J. Heyworth Dunne, pp. 108, 147–8, 199, 204, under his full name على بن هارون بن علان اليهودى الجهبذ and who was killed in 940/941 in Baghdād. In *Ecl.*, iii, p. 282, a Jewish banker named Abū 'Ali b. Faḍlān (اليهودى) of Baghdād (998) refused to grant a loan (قرض) to the Emīr Bahā' ad-Daula, which led to an attack on Jews in order to extort money from them. In *Ibn al-Athīr*, vol. x, 14, 79, we hear of a Jewish tax-farmer of Basra, Ibn 'Allān al-yahūdi, ابن علان اليهودى ضامن البصرة who served the Caliphs for more than twenty years. He was extremely wealthy and granted a loan of 100,000 dīnārs to Niẓām al-Mulk. As a result of intrigues he was murdered in 1079. He was deeply mourned in his city, and the Sulṭān himself bewailed him for three days. Another Jewish contemporary of Niẓām al-Mulk, who occupied an important official position, was a certain Abū Sa'd b. Samḥa al-yahūdi, ابو سعد بن سمحا اليهودى, who resided in Baghdād in 1091 and was an agent of Malik Shāh (*Ibn al-Athīr*, x, 123–4). In the Ottoman Empire we frequently meet with Jewish bankers and brokers to the Pashas of Baghdād. But that lies beyond the scope of this study. These instances are no more than a few gleanings from Arab sources regarding Jewish commercial activity. A further and systematic investigation is one of the desiderata of Jewish historical research.

3. The Jewish Court Bankers in the Light of Gaonic Literature

1.

With the help of these Arab sources and in the light of the data they furnish, we shall now proceed to demonstrate in a particular instance how the Arab sources may contribute to the elucidation of concrete problems in Jewish history, and how a knowledge and understanding of events in Jewish history based only on Hebrew sources may be supplemented by contemporary Arab chronicles.

In 1910 L. Ginzberg published a Geniza fragment [1] from the Oxford collection of manuscripts, of which we quote the following [2] :—

וכן כל חפץ ושאלה אשר יהיה לכם מצד
המלכות הגד תגידוהו לפנינו כי אז נצוה
את בעלי בתים חשובים אשר בבגדד אשר
אנחנו יושבים בינידם בני מ"ר נטירא ובני
מ"ר אהרן זכר הנאספים לברכה וזכרון פליטידם
דקימה ואז ישיבו לכם מאת המלך כאשר
יספיק יי"י מעזנו בידם כן תעשו ואל תטשו.

Ginzberg's rendering of the passage is :—

"And thus whenever you have transactions with the Government, I admonish you to let us know about them, that we may consult with the prominent members of the Baghdād community in the midst of which we dwell, namely, the sons of R. Neṭīra and the sons of R. Aaron . . . and then the Government [3] will deal with you according as the Lord will aid your helpers. Thus do ye and not otherwise."

The task set by the publication of this fragment was to find out the author and thereby the historical position of that

[1] *Geonica* (Geniza-Studies), New York, 1910, ii, pp. 87–8.

[2] Cf. also *Iggeret R. Scherira Gaon*, ed. B. Lewin, Haifa, 1921, p. xxv, with slight emendations.

[3] Egypt was still a province of the 'Abbāsid empire then, and thus subject to the central government in Baghdād.

document, and to identify the prominent Jewish personalities named in it, so far as the available data permitted.

The problem of the authorship gave rise to numerous suppositions. L. Ginzberg [1] himself thought that R. Joseph, R. Saadya's opponent, was the author ; J. Mann [2] attributed the fragment to R. Neḥemia, the Gaon of Pumbadita. On the other hand, H. Malter [3] attributed it to R. Dosa, the son of R. Saadya Gaon. Finally, J. N. Epstein [4] recognized, in the light of another document (published by D. Revel) [5] in 1923 under the title *Iggeret Rab Saadja Gaon*, that the author of Ginzberg's Geniza fragment was no other than R. Saadya Gaon al-Fayyūmi, who must have sent this letter shortly after his assumption of the Gaonate, i.e. in 928, from Baghdād to Egypt.[6]

In effect this opinion of Epstein was brilliantly confirmed by another Geniza fragment published in the following year (1924) by B. Lewin [7] from the collection of manuscripts of Isr. Lévi (Paris). The identity of handwriting and number of lines to the page (nineteen), as well as linguistic and stylistic reasons,[8] alone sufficed to indicate that this fragment ("L") and "G" were from one and the same manuscript. But in addition the following Arabic words were to be found at the beginning of "L" as heading :—

... כ[תא]ב ראס אלמתיבה̈ אלפיומי ז"ל
[כ]תבה בבגדאד פי וקת אן ולי אלראסה (אלריאסה̈?)
[רסא?]לה אלי אהל מצר.

[1] Ibid., ii, pp. 422–3.

[2] *JQR.*, vii (1916–17), p. 467.

[3] *R. Saadia Gaon, his Life and his Works*, Philadelphia, 1922, p. 113.

[4] *Debir* (דביר), a Hebrew quarterly of Jewish science, ed. I. Elbogen, J. N. Epstein, and H. Torczyner, Berlin, 1923, i, p. 189.

[5] *Debir*, ibid., i, pp. 180–8.

[6] *Debir*, ibid., p. 190.

[7] *Ginze Kedem* (גנזי קדם), ed. B. Lewin, Haifa, 1923, ii, p. 34.

[8] Ibid., ii, p. 33, line 17, like the Ginzberg fragment, makes mention of בעלי בתים חשובים ונכבדים אשר בבגדד, which is a further evidence for the homogeneity of "G" and "L".

("Letter of Fayyūmi, of blessed memory, Head of the Academy (i.e. Gaon), written by him in Baghdād at the time of his appointment to the Headship as an epistle unto the people of Misr (i.e. Fusṭāṭ).")[1]

Thus sender, time, place, and addressee were defined in all their particulars, and the question of the authorship of Ginzberg's Geniza fragment was answered.

2.

Ever since the publication of "G" the specialists have laboured to find an answer to the other question too, namely: Who were these "prominent members of the Baghdād community", those "Bne Neṭīra" and "Bne Aaron" that were able to make representations to the Court, and to intercede on behalf of their co-religionists?[2]

With regard to the "Bne Neṭīra" we possess information from other Jewish sources. In a Geniza fragment published by Harkavy,[3] as well as in the Hebrew[4] and Arabic[5] report

[1] J. N. Epstein in *Debir*, 1924, ii, p. 325; cf. also B. Lewin in *Ginze Kedem*, ii, p. 34, and now J. Mann, *Texts and Studies*, p. 67.

[2] S. Assaf (*Enc. Jud.*, vol. vii, p. 275, s.v. Geonim) says: "Die Geonim bemühten sich auch durch Vermittlung hoffähiger Juden Bagdads wie Netira und seine Söhne auf die Judenpolitik des Chalifenhofes Einfluss zu gewinnen." He does not, however, mention the "Bne Aaron". On the other hand, see D. S. Sassoon (*Enc. Jud.*, vol. iii, p. 957), s.v. Bagdad: "Unter den Juden in Bagdad zeichneten sich in der gaonäischen Zeit die Familien Mar Netira und Mar Aaron aus, die der Regierung nahe standen und um das Wohl der Juden in Bagdad und in anderen Provinzen bemüht waren."

[3] Published under the title *Netira und seine Söhne: eine angesehene jüdische Familie in Bagdad im Anfang des* 10 *Jahrhunderts* (Festschrift für A. Berliner, 1903, Hebrew part, pp. 34–43). Cf. hereto the additions and emendations of S. Fraenkel, *JQR.*, xvii (1905), pp. 386–8. Regarding J. Friedländer's hypothesis about the identity of the author of this Harkavy fragment with the Arabic report of Nathan Hababli, and his opinion that both fragments were parts of a lost History of Baghdād (*JQR.*, xvii, 1905, pp. 747–760), cf. A. Marx, "Der arabische Bustanai Bericht und Nathan Hababli," in *Livre d'Hommage à la mémoire de S. Poznanski*, Warsaw, 1927, pp. 76–81.

[4] Ed. A. Neubauer, *Mediæval Jewish Chronicles*, Oxford, 1895, ii, p. 78, l. 5, last; p. 79, l. 11. On Nathan Hababli, cf. Ginzberg, *Geonica*, i, 22–36.

[5] J. Friedländer, "The Arabic Original of the Report of R. Nathan Hababli," *JQR.*, xvii (1905), pp. 747–761.

of Nathan Hababli, *Neṭīra*, the father, figures as one of the leading Jewish notables [1] of Baghdād towards the end of the ninth century (the reign of al-Mu'taḍid and his successors), who was in a position to influence the Caliph's decisions [2] in favour of his party in an internal dispute in the Jewish community.[3] The same sources, especially Harkavy's fragment, also give us particulars about the " *Bne* Neṭīra ", the sons, who are called Sahl and Isḥāq. Sahl, the elder, succeeded to his father in business and occupied, together with his brother Isḥāq,[4] the same social and political position as he had. Like their father, the Bne Neṭīra are represented as influential personalities, who in an internal dispute of the Jewish community secured a decision of the Caliph in favour of their candidate for the Gaonate.[5]

In any case, the " Bne Neṭīra " of these sources certainly answer to the description " of prominent members of the Baghdād community " which is applied to them in Saadya's fragment, and possessed the influence in court circles which that document ascribes to them.

We do not, however, find in these Jewish sources any

[1] Both reports of Nathan Hababli also mention a Joseph b. Phineas as one of the Baghdād notables who acted together with Neṭīra.

[2] *Vide* Neubauer, ii, 79–80 ; Friedländer, ibid., ii, 1, 13 ; for details thereon v. Graetz, *Geschichte*, vol. v, 4th edition, pp. 446 ff. ; Dubnow, *Weltgeschichte*, vol. iii, p. 474 ; A. Marx and L. Margolis, *History of the Jewish People*, p. 269.

[3] To what Neṭīra's influence was due we know from the extremely enlightening Geniza fragment published by Harkavy, which gives us an interesting insight into the inner life of the Jewish community of Baghdād in general. It seems that al-Mu'taḍid appointed Neṭīra to be collector of the Jews' poll-tax (Harkavy, ibid., p. 36). Opinion differs as to the official position in virtue of which the poll-tax was collected. Cf. Graetz, *Geschichte*, v, pp. 131, 435 ; cf., however, J. Mann, *JQR.*, x, 1919, pp. 123 ff. Perhaps he was a *jahbadh*, an office which was, according to Ibn Taghribirdi, ii, 174, as we have seen, the one which the Jews might occupy.

[4] The Harkavy fragment ends just where one hoped to find dètails regarding the nature of their joint business.

[5] The candidate of the Bne Neṭīra was R. Saadya. Nathan Hababli states expressly that Saadya was victorious because those Bne Neṭīra and other rich Jews of Baghdād were on his side and influenced the Caliph al-Muqtadir (ed. Neubauer, ii, 79).

mention of persons whom we could equate with the "Bne Aaron". Regarding their identity the most divergent views have been expressed. L. Ginzberg,[1] also H. Malter [2] thought that in this fragment Aaron b. Sarjado was Mar Aaron, the father of the Bne Aaron. Whilst, however, Aaron b. Sarjado was a very prominent and influential personality and Gaon of Pumbadita [3] (943–960), this identification is precluded by chronological circumstances of which Ginzberg could not know at the time; namely that, as we have seen, the document which presupposes the death of Mar Aaron was sent by R. Saadya Gaon in the year 928, whereas this Aaron lived until 960.

J. Mann was especially zealous in his endeavours to identify the "Bne Aaron" on the basis of data furnished by further Geniza material. This zeal, however, carried him too far; for whenever he came across the name of "Aaron" or "Bne Aaron", for the most part such as flourished between 945 and 960 C.E., or whenever he found a prominent personality of the same period mentioned, he thought he had struck upon the trail of the Aaron family of our Saadya fragment. This led to rather contradictory theories which did not advance the cause.[4]

Now that it has been established that the Saadya letter, in which the "Bne Aaron" are mentioned, was written in 928, all the conjectures connecting the "Bne Aaron" with

[1] *Geonica*, ii, p. 87.

[2] *R. Saadia Gaon*, p. 133 n.

[3] About him, v. Graetz, v, 4 ed., p. 293, and H. Malter, ibid., s.v. He was one of the sharpest opponents of R. Saadya Gaon, and therefore it would be very improbable to think of his sons, who, by the way, are mentioned nowhere, though they would have been helpful to the Egyptian friends of R. Saadya. J. Mann has also other reasons for rejecting Ginzberg's explanation. Cf. *REJ.*, 73 (1921), p. 109; *JQR.*, viii (1917–18), p. 34.

[4] Cf. J. Mann, *JQR.*, viii (1917–18), pp. 342 ff., 346, 347, "probably identical with the Bne Aaron, the influential grandees of Baghdad"; *Geonic Studies*, Hebrew Union College Jubilee Volume, Cincinnati, 1925, p. 231; cf. *JQR.*, ix (1918–19), p. 156; *Texts and Studies*, p. 78. In view of the frequency of the name Aaron in Babylonian Jewry at this period chronology is the sole determining factor.

persons that lived so much later are disposed of. The question as to the identity of the "Bne Aaron" must therefore be taken up anew, but this I shall endeavour to do from an entirely different angle.

3.

As neither the Geniza fragments published hitherto nor any other Hebrew sources [1] could help us further in our search for the "Bne Aaron" or their father, it is necessary to turn to contemporary Arab sources.

This requirement is all the more reasonable as applied to Arab sources dealing with events that took place in Baghdād and the eastern provinces of the ʿAbbāsid Empire, particularly in an age of such importance as that of the Gaonate.

Why should not persons like the "Bne Aaron" and "Bne Neṭīra", who are expressly stated to have had access to the Court, have left some record of their names and activities in the Arab chronicles of that period? In effect, as we shall see, the solution to our problem lies just here. The מלך (king) of Saadya's letter, who reigned at the time of these "Bne Aaron" and "Bne Neṭīra" and who maintained relations with them, was no other than the Caliph al-Muqtadir.

Now the Arab sources, with which we have been dealing all along, embrace the reign of this sovereign; that they tell of some influential Jews we have already seen. I now wish to make the assertion that the two bankers and Court-Jews, Joseph b. Phineas and Aaron b. Amram, are closely connected with the "prominent members of the Baghdād community" of whom Saadya speaks; and more

[1] It must be remarked that J. Mann, in his *Texts and Studies*, p. 70, does not offer any new opinion relative to the "Bne Aaron" problem. He only remarks on our Saadya letter: "Interesting is his promise to his correspondents in Egypt that their political requests would be taken care of in Baghdad by the influential sons of Netira and of Aaron who would intervene on their behalf at the seat of the government." Cf., however, p. 78, and now *Tarbiz*, Jerusalem, 1934, pp. 148 ff.

particularly that Aaron b. Amram—to start with him—is no other than the long-sought father of the " Bne Aaron ".

In order to achieve a demonstration which can claim methodical correctness, I shall briefly recapitulate what conditions of time, place, social status, etc., must be satisfied by those whose identity with the " prominent members of the Baghdād community " in the Saadya fragment is alleged.

(1) They must have been resident in Baghdād.[1]

(2) They must have been in direct relations with Baghdād governmental circles, which enabled them to intervene on behalf of their brethren (even those from other provinces) before the Caliph.

(3) They must already have held an influential position in 928, at the time of the Caliph al-Muqtadir.[2]

(4) They must have been indebted to their fathers[3] for their high office.[4]

(5) At the time when this letter was written, i.e. in 928, their fathers, Mar Neṭīra and Mar Aaron, could not have been any longer alive.[5]

(6) " Bne Neṭīra " and " Bne Aaron " must have been contemporaries.[6]

(7) They must also have been partisans of R. Saadya.[7]

[1] This feature precludes any attempt to identify them with personalities residing elsewhere.

[2] The letter of R. Saadya was written in 928.

[3] The " Bne Neṭīra " and " Bne Aaron " seem to have been influential only in virtue of their being heirs of a position held by their fathers. They were just the " sons of their fathers " and are therefore called " *Bne* Neṭīra " and " *Bne* Aaron " without further specification.

[4] The text gives the impression that we have here to do with purely mundane personalities, prominent in politics or business, and not with Talmudic celebrities.

[5] Note the phrase זכר הנאספים לברכה.

[6] The fact that the two families are mentioned together as they are, is an important chronological indication that has hitherto not been taken into account. It teaches us that only contemporaries of the " Bne Neṭīra " can be identified with the " Bne Aaron ".

[7] Apart from the fact that R. Saadya was obviously on cordial terms with them, we have direct evidence that Sahl b. Neṭīra was a pupil of his. Cf. Harkavy, ibid., pp. 38, 40.

That the Aaron b. Amram of the Arab writings with which we have been dealing satisfies all the conditions for the father of the " Bne Aaron " can be seen at a glance. He lived in Baghdād. He had close relations with the highest Government circles. He was Court Banker for many years between 908 and 924 (he is not heard of at any later date). He was obviously the right man to intercede before the Caliph on behalf of his co-religionists. It is true that only one son of his receives mention in Arabic sources as having appeared at Court in connection with his father's functions as *jahbadh*.[1] But all the sons and some other members of the families of Joseph b. Phineas and Aaron b. Amram were collectively included under the designation " successors ", " heirs ", and " representatives ".

There remains, therefore, only the test of dates: Were the children of this Aaron b. Amram contemporary with the " Bne Neṭīra " ?

4.

We have already seen from the report of Nathan Hababli that the " Bne Neṭīra " lived at the time of the Caliph

[1] Comparison of *Misk.*, 112, and *Misk.*, 128, shows that this " Ibn Aaron " was probably called Bishr. About the name Bishr b. Aaron there is a lack of clarity in the Arab sources. There is an Abū Naṣr Bishr b. Aaron, who is expressly called " the Christian secretary " (cf. e.g. *Ṭabari*, 1511, 1524; *Tan.*, i, 52; *Wuz.*, 33, 159, 243), and a Bishr b. Aaron without any qualification, who is probably the son of our Aaron b. Amram. The index to the *Eclipse of the Abbasid Caliphate*, s.v. Bishr, does not clear the matter up. The *jahbadh* of the Vizier Ibn al-Furāt was Aaron b. Amram; the index, however, attributes the same function also to a Bishr b. Aaron. This is hardly to be explained otherwise than by assuming that this Bishr is a son of Aaron b. Amram who, as we have seen in *Misk.*, 128, appears at court on business with his father. If this is so, there is a considerable amount of probability in favour of identifying him further with Bishr b. Aaron, the father-in-law of Aaron b. Joseph Sarjado who, according to Jewish sources, subsequently undertook to play the part of mediator between the Saadyan party, to whom in that case his own family the " Bne Aaron " belonged, and their bitter opponents of whom his son-in-law was the most influential and wealthy. This probability is certainly not weakened by the description of Bishr b. Aaron in the Jewish sources as an exceedingly rich and prominent person. Cf. Neubauer, *Mediaeval Jewish Chronicles*, ii, pp. 80 ff.; J. Mann, *JQR.*, xi, N.S., p. 426; ix, p. 156 n.; *Enc. Jud.*, i, p. 56, s.v. Aaron b. Joseph ha-Kohen Sarjado.

al-Muqtadir and played an important part at his court. Now at the very same time the Arab sources show us Aaron b. Amram and his sons occupying a similar position. We should therefore have expected to find in the Arab sources, that have proved so rich in data on Aaron b. Amram, some particulars about his contemporaries, the Neṭīra family. However, the Arab sources accessible to-day do not mention any Neṭīra, and an "Ibn Neṭīra" only in another connection.[1] On the other hand, as has been shown, another Jewish personality is constantly mentioned together with Aaron b. Amram, namely Joseph b. Phineas. The latter also bore the title of *jahbadh*, held the same privileged position at the court of the Caliph al-Muqtadir, and helped, together with Aaron b. Amram, to supply the Caliph's pecuniary needs. Might this Joseph b. Phineas perhaps have had something to do with the "Bne Neṭīra"?

This question can now be answered with the help of our Jewish sources in an unequivocally affirmative fashion. For these sources, which supplement the Arab ones on that very point, likewise mention our Joseph b. Phineas as an important and influential personality, and, moreover, furnish us with the further information that he used his influence with the Caliph on behalf of Babylonian Jewry, *together with one Neṭīra*: the very same Neṭīra of whose activities I have already spoken, and whose sons the "Bne Neṭīra" are mentioned by Saadya. Furthermore, the Jewish sources state explicitly the relationship that existed between Joseph b. Phineas and Neṭīra. In the Hebrew report[2] of Nathan Hababli we hear of יוסף בן פינחס וחתנו נטירא "Joseph b. Phineas

[1] The Sahl b. Naẓīr, mentioned in *Misk.*, 349 and 379, who acted as *jahbadh* to the governor Barīdī in Ahwāz (936), is perhaps identical with our Sahl b. Neṭīra of Baghdād. The Harkavy fragment tells us that Sahl b. Neṭīra had in Fārs a bazār or market that yielded him 2,000 dirham a day; this might be taken as an indication of some connection between them. It is not unlikely that after the Caliph al-Muqtadir's death business interests led him to Ahwāz, where he became *jahbadh* to al-Barīdi. The story of his cruel death at the hand of al-Barīdi is related in *Misk.*, 379.

[2] *Nathan Hababli*, ed. Neubauer, ii, 78.

and his son-in-law Neṭīra ", and in the Arabic report [1] more detailed יוסף בן פינחס וכתנה זוג אבנתה נטירא אבו סהל ואסחאק " Joseph b. Phineas and his son-in-law, the husband of his daughter, Neṭīra, father of Sahl and Isḥāq ".

Thus we see that Joseph b. Phineas was Neṭīra's father-in-law, and so the grandfather of the " Bne Neṭīra ".

This important statement regarding the kinship between Neṭīra and Joseph b. Phineas permits us to recognize a remarkable correspondence of personalities between the Arabic and Hebrew literary sources of the tenth century.

Just as the Arab sources represent Joseph b. Phineas and Aaron b. Amram [2] as joint holders of the same high office, so, on the other hand, the Saadya letter speaks of the " Bne Neṭīra " and " Bne Aaron " as of contemporaries who acted together in virtue of the same high degree of influence at court.[3] The parallel is too obvious to leave any room for doubt; the Arab sources speak of the father and the grandfather, the Hebrew ones of the sons and the grandsons.

The parallel would, of course, have been more striking still

[1] J. Friedländer, *JQR.*, xvii (1905), p. 747, text recto i, l. 9–10.

[2] Having established that the father of the " Bne Aaron " of the Hebrew sources was in all probability Aaron b. Amram, one naturally asks whether the Jewish sources of that period make any mention of an " Aaron b. Amram " with whom he might be identified. As a matter of fact, the name of a highly respected Aaron b. Amram does occur in an epistle of the Palestinian Ben Mēīr of the year 921. Cf. *Enc. Jud.*, iv, pp. 64–70, s.v. Ben Meir. Cf. Eppenstein, " Beiträge zur gaonäischen Literatur," *MGWJ.*, 1913, pp. 455–6; Graetz, vol. v, 4th ed., p. 447, n. 1; S. Schechter, *Saadyana*, Cambridge, 1903, p. 20, and above all, J. Ch. Bornstein in *Sefer ha-jobel likebod N. Sokolow*, Warsaw, 1904, p. 105.

[3] The connection between the Court-Jews of the Arab sources and the בעלי בתים חשובים of the Saadya letter gives us an answer to the question asked above regarding the concrete position which the " Bne Neṭīra " and " Bne Aaron " might have held at court. Apparently they held the office of *jahbadh*, working in the banking firm founded by their father and their grandfather. They were considered as their legal heirs, to whom the Vizier ʿAli b. ʿĪsā alludes as the " successors " and " heirs ". The family connections of prominent Jews in that age support the suggestion that the family of the " Bne Neṭīra " and the " Bne Aaron " were later on allied by marriage as well.

if the Arab sources had named "Neṭīra" instead of Joseph b. Phineas. It seems, however, that Joseph b. Phineas outlived his son-in-law Neṭīra, and continued the latter's business together with his grandsons, the "Bne Netīra". It is not impossible that it was Neṭīra's death which induced his father-in-law, Joseph b. Phineas, to go into partnership with the merchant and banker Aaron b. Amram, whose social and communal position was similar to his own, in order to carry on the business of his family more easily.

If, therefore, Saadya considered the heirs of these magnates the most suitable advocates of Jewish causes at the Royal Court, it was thanks to their position and functions, of which, with the help of contemporary Arab sources, we have been able to reconstruct, we hope, a picture essentially accurate.

B. UNDER THE FĀṬIMID CALIPHATE

I. YA'QŪB B. KILLIS

1.

IN our survey of the sources for data on the position of the Jews in the political and economic life of Mediaeval Islam we are led from Baghdād to Cairo at the court of the Fāṭimides. Our attention is arrested by a name which recurs in almost all the Arabic histories of tenth century Egypt, and which posterity still remembers as that of the first vizier of the Fāṭimid dynasty in Egypt.[1] This personality Abū'l-Faraj Ya'qūb b. Yūsuf b. Killis—or simply Ya'qūb b. Killis [2]—deserves to be made the subject of a special inquiry, not only because the deeds and achievements of this statesman afford a unique insight into the administrative machinery and economic fabric of the Egypt of his times, but also because his life brings into relief the important part played by a Jew in the establishment of the Fāṭimid dynasty in the Nile Valley. In Ya'qūb b. Killis we meet one of those border-line figures which, born in a purely Jewish milieu, derive such extraordinary abilities thence as to attain to positions of supreme importance in the Muslim state to whose service these gifts are then devoted.

Whereas the Jewish court bankers under the Caliph al-Muqtadir in Baghdād were able, by means of their financial assistance, to exercise a retarding influence upon the *decline* of the 'Abbāsid Empire, Ya'qūb b. Killis, on the other hand,

[1] For the sources on the rule of the Fāṭimids in Egypt and on the relations of the sources to one another and on the problems of Fāṭimid historiography in general cf., besides the introductions of the respective editors, specially C. H. Beckers's basic work, " Zur Geschichtsschreibung unter den Fatimiden," in his *Beiträge z. Geschichte Aegyptens unter dem Islam*, Strassburg, 1902, i, 1–31. See also E. Blochet in *Rev. Orient. Latin*, vi, 455–487.

[2] His full name is ابو الفرج يعقوب بن يوسف بن كلّس. A Christian source calls him ابن خلس ; cf. *Histoire d'Abraham le Syrien*, p. 382.

was privileged to play a leading part in the laying of the economic and political foundations for a *new* state, that of the Fāṭimids in Egypt.

Early Years in Palestine

The only dependable fact preserved regarding the early life of Ya'qūb b. Killis is his Jewish parentage and his Baghdād origin.

He was born of Jewish parents in 318/930 [1] at Baghdād, and is always referred to by the Arab historians [2] as "a Jew of the people of Baghdād", "a Baghdād Jew", or "a Jewish clerk". He received his early education in Baghdād [3] and migrated from there to Syria with his father at a tender age. The exact date of this event is not known. It is certain that they settled in ar-Ramla (Palestine), where Ya'qūb probably went into business for the first time. The sources differ regarding the nature of his occupation. According to Ibn Taghribirdi [4] he practised there as a broker; according to other sources he was an "agent of the merchants" (وكيل التجار).[5] It is stated that he was "honest in his dealings with the tradespeople"; yet fortune did not smile upon him. He failed and, not being able to meet his obligations, fled from ar-Ramla to Egypt.

The sources do not enable us to determine the exact date of Ya'qūb b. Killis's arrival in Egypt. Ibn Khallikān [6] believes that it took place in the year 942–3, but that is highly

[1] This date is given by Ibn 'Asākir (quoted by *Ibn Khallikān*, ii, 443). According to *Ibn Khallikān*, ii, 440, he traced his lineage to Moses and Aaron; or, according to another view (ibid.), to the kindred of the pre-Islamic poet as-Samau'al b. 'Ādiyā al-yahūdi.

[2] *Ibn Qalānisi*, p. 31: يهودى من اهل بغداد. Also *Maqrīzi*, ii, 5; *Ibn Taghribirdi*, ii, 45; *adh-Dhahabi*, i, p. 180; *Ibn aṣ-Ṣairafi*, p. 94; *Ibn Khallikān*, ii, 442.

[3] *Ibn Khallikān*, ii, 440.

[4] *Ibn Taghrib.*, ii, 45.

[5] *Maqrīzi*, ii, 5; *Ibn Qalānisi*, p. 33; *Ibn aṣ-Ṣairafi*, p. 94; *Yaḥyā b. Sa'īd*, ed. Cheikho, p. 172; ed. Kratchk., p. 433.

[6] Op. cit., ii, 442.

improbable. All that can be said with certainty is, that Ya'qūb b. Killis was already present at the court of Kāfūr, the ruler of Egypt,[1] in the year 355/966, and it may be presumed that he had been living in Egypt for some years prior to that date.

With Kāfūr in Egypt

At any rate, Ya'qūb b. Killis succeeded in establishing himself after only a brief sojourn in Fusṭāṭ. As in ar-Ramla, he began as a merchant,[2] and in this capacity soon entered into business relations with Kāfūr, for whom he discharged various commissions. He thus rose rapidly to the position of a sort of purveyor to the court, and became known as a " merchant of Kāfūr ".[3]

We gain a valuable insight into the economic and financial organization of the country from the information that Kāfūr paid for the wares delivered by Ya'qūb b. Killis not in cash but in orders on villages or estates of Egypt. As a result Ya'qūb b. Killis had to make frequent visits to these various estates and so grew familiar with rural conditions (اخبار القرى). He soon became the recognized authority on the agricultural situation, and is stated by Maqrīzi always to have been ready with reliable information " when questioned on the state or extent of the crops in the districts, or on the internal or external affairs of the villages ".[4] Thanks to this qualification his undertakings flourished, and he began to accumulate wealth.

All this time, it appears, he had been dealing only indirectly with the court. However, his reputation for ability, cleverness, and trustworthiness reached Kāfūr himself, who " was astonished by it ".[4] It would seem that Kāfūr was looking for just such a man in order to take him into the service of the state. Be that as it may, his official

[1] Cf. *Enc. Isl.*, s.v. Kāfūr.

[2] *Yaḥyā b. Sa'īd*, ed. Cheikho, p. 172 ; ed. Kratchkovsky, p. 433.

[3] *Ibn Khallikān*, ii, 443 ; *Ibn Taghrib.*, ii, 45.

[4] *Maqrīzi*, ii, 5.

position at court and in the administration dates, if one is to believe Ibn aṣ-Ṣairafī, from the following incident.[1]

A Jewish acquaintance of Ya'qūb b. Killis informed him that a sum of 20,000 dīnārs lay buried on the premises of Ibn Baladi (b. Bekr), a merchant of ar-Ramla. According to Islamic law the estate of a person who dies without relatives belongs to the state. Ya'qūb b. Killis wrote to Kāfūr about the buried treasure and offered, with his knowledge of the place, to find and bring it. Kāfūr gave his approval and provided mules for the transport of the money. Just at this time news came of the death of the merchant Bukīr b. Aaron, whose estate Ya'qūb b. Killis was likewise commissioned to investigate; also of the death of a Jew of al-Farma, who possessed large supplies of cord. On investigating the latter he found it to be worth 20,000 dīnārs, which he promptly realized. Then he proceeded to ar-Ramla. The search in the dwelling of Ibn Baladi brought not 20,000 but 30,000 dīnārs to light, whereupon he wrote Kāfūr: "O Ustādh, I knew only of 20,000 dīnārs; now I have found 30,000"; and Kāfūr's confidence in him was greatly strengthened. An investigation of Ibn Aaron's effects likewise yielded a rich monetary harvest, which again confirmed him in Kāfūr's favour. Kāfūr sent him a large share of the money, but Ya'qūb returned all but 1,000 dīnārs, saying, "That is enough for me." This act was also highly commended by Kāfūr.[2] The result was that Kāfūr conceived such a high regard for him that he used to ask his advice in all his economic and political affairs. A man who acted as permanent advisor to the head of the state must have done so in some official capacity. The sources, however, seem to be at variance with each other regarding its nature. Ibn aṣ-Ṣairafi [1] has "Comptroller of the Dīwān for Syria and Egypt", which he was left to administer as he saw fit. Ibn Khallikān, on the other hand, places him in charge of the "Dīwān al-Khāṣṣ".[2] In any case, the office

[1] *Ibn aṣ-Ṣairafi*, p. 94.

[2] *Ibn Khallikān*, ii, 441.

must have been an exceedingly important one, carrying with it the control of the entire financial administration. This can be inferred from the fact that Kāfūr issued special instructions to all the other dīwāns to refrain from incurring even the smallest expenditure without an order from Ya'qūb b. Killis. Maqrīzi also asserts that everything went through his hands. His exceptional position at the court of Kāfūr and his wide powers and influence are further apparent from the deference with which he was treated on all sides : even the chamberlains and shereefs stood up to do him honour.[1]

Conversion to Islam

Hitherto Judaism had not been a hindrance to his advance on the path of fame, position, influence, and respect. He was known as a Jew and remained one. "All this," Ibn 'Asākir assures us after tracing Ya'qūb b. Killis's career up to this juncture, "whilst abiding by his religion," whilst adhering to his Jewish faith.[2]

However, a change in Kāfūr's attitude toward him now set in. Kāfūr, after such long experience of Ya'qūb's prudence, disinterestedness,[3] and political foresight, seems to have contemplated making him vizier. One of his intimates relates that, referring with pride and gratification to Ibn Killis, Kāfūr exclaimed : "What vizier could compare with him ?" [4] The fact that he was a Jew was, however, an obstacle to the attainment of this point, and many of the sources have handed down the sentence of Kāfūr : "Were he (Ya'qūb b. Killis) a Muslim, he would be the right man for vizier." [5]

These words and the all too tempting prospect of the vizierate did not fail to have their effect on Ibn Killis, and he

[1] *Maqrīzi*, ii, 5.

[2] *Ibn Khallikān*, ii, 443.

[3] *Ibn Khall.*, ii, 440, adds : "His mind was not set upon money-making. When Kāfūr sent him money he sent it back, retaining only his expenses."

[4] *Ibn aṣ-Ṣairafi*, p. 94.

[5] *Ibn Taghribirdi*, ii, 45 ; *Maqrīzi*, ii, 6 : ولو كان مسلما لصلح ان يكون وزيرا.

declared himself a Muslim. Whether the renunciation of the religion of his fathers cost Ya'qūb many pangs or not, it is certain that the sources make the above saying of Kāfūr's, that is to say, worldly ambition rather than conviction, the motive for his conversion. As " his spirit longed for dominion " and " he aspired to the vizierate ",[1] he facilitated his rise in office by adopting Islam.[2]

The sources add various ornamental details to the story of his conversion. He is said to have taken a sheikh into his house to teach him Qur'ān, Fiqh, and other Islamic sciences ; finally, on a Friday, he entered a mosque for the first time, and thereby openly confessed the Muslim faith. Then, escorted by a large number of people, he rode to Kāfūr, who was very gratified at Ya'qūb's conversion and honoured him with a robe (خلع) and other gifts. Maqrīzi also speaks of a state reception to which all the *ahl ad-daula* came to congratulate him.[3]

Despite all the honours showered upon Ya'qūb b. Killis after his conversion and his advancement by Kāfūr to a higher rank,[4] the chief consequence was the aggravated enmity of the vizier Abu'l-Faḍl Ja'far b. al-Furāt.[5] This enmity was of far-reaching effect, for it compelled Ya'qūb to flee the country and thus brought him into contact with the Court of the Fāṭimids in Maghrib.

Ibn al-Furāt had long been viewing with misgiving and envy the repeated and growing favours which Kāfūr kept lavishing on Ibn Killis. Now that the latter had become

[1] *Ibn Khallikān*, ii, 441.

[2] The sources differ regarding the date of conversion. *Ibn aṣ-Ṣairafi*, p. 92, gives the year 350/962 ; *Maqrīzi*, ii, 5, and *Ibn Khallikān*, l.c., 356/967, which is the most probable. Yaḥyā b. Sa'īd and others state only : ثم اسلم في ايام كافور. The sources make frequent mention also of Christian officials at that time who turned to Islam formally in order to advance in the political career. Cf. also C. H. Becker, *Islamstudien*, i, p. 154.

[3] *Ibn aṣ-Ṣairafi*, p. 94.

[4] *Maqrīzi*, ii, 5 ; *Ibn Khallikān*, ii, 442.

[5] On this vizier cf. *Enc. Isl.* ; *Ibn Khallikān*, i, 137.

eligible for the vizierate, his ill-will towards him was heightened.[1] His opportunity came when Kāfūr, Ya'qūb's powerful patron, died in 968, leaving him exposed to his enemies. Ibn al-Furāt promptly had all the secretaries and heads of dīwāns,[2] including Ya'qūb b. Killis, arrested, and imposed heavy fines upon them. According to Ibn Khallikān he was subjected to extortions until he found means to buy his freedom and flee from Egypt to Maghrib.[3]

With al-Mu'izz in Maghrib

As it turned out, therefore, Ya'qūb b. Killis's conversion to Islam had quite another result from that expected. That he had been an opportunist appears from the sources, which expressly state that upon his arrival in Maghrib he again associated himself with the Jews, who were in sympathy with al-Mu'izz.[4]

Once under Fāṭimid rule his religion made no difference; for the well-known tolerance of this dynasty towards the *ahl adh-Dhimma* made it possible for a Jew to attain to the highest position in the state. Ya'qūb b. Killis entered the service of al-Mu'izz in 357/968 and began a new phase.[5]

[1] *Ibn Khallikān*, ii, 440; *Maqrīzi*, ii, 5, adds that Ya'qūb b. Killis feared the vizier.

[2] *Ibn Khallikān*, i, 137; cf. *Yaḥyā b. Sa'īd*, ed. Kratchkowsky, p. 811; ed. Cheikho, p. 129.

[3] According to *Maqrīzi*, ii, 6, he realized the danger which menaced him from Ibn al-Furāt betimes, and fled the country while Kāfūr was still alive. But this can hardly be right. According to *Ibn Khallikān*, ii, 440, Ya'qūb b. Killis borrowed money from his brother in order to flee to Maghrib. This brother's name is given in Maqrīzi: *Itti'āẓ*, p. 144, Abū Ibrāhīm Sahl b. Killis. He was one of the nobles executed by al-Ḥākim in 394/1004. This fact would seem to imply that he had remained a Jew, as almost all those executed belonged to the ahl adh-Dhimma. The sources also mention a daughter of Ya'qūb b. Killis, who married a certain Yārūkh, probably Bārūkh, as given in *Yaḥyā b. Sa'īd*, ed. Cheikho, p. 220. Cf. *Maqrīzi*, ii, 8.

[4] Ibn 'Asākir apud *Ibn Khallikān*, ii, 443: هرب الى المغرب واتّصل بيهود; *Ibn Qalānisi*, p. 33: قصد يهودا كانوا هناك مع المعزّ.

[5] All the sources agree in stating that Ya'qūb b. Killis fled in 357/968 to the court of the 'Ubaydite ruler al-Mu'izz in Maghrib. According to one view cited by *Ibn Khallikān*, l.c., he had encountered the General

In what did Ya'qūb b. Killis's activities in Maghrib consist ? We know that he remained there for five years, 968–973, but the sources are reticent about his doings during that period. They tell us only that he left for Maghrib and entered the service of the Caliph al-Mu'izz.[1] Ibn Taghribirdi alone adds a very interesting fact to our knowledge. According to him Ya'qūb b. Killis fled to Maghrib and became no more and no less than "*one of the important factors in inducing al-Mu'izz to send Jauhar to Egypt.*"[2] He thus ascribes to Ya'qūb nothing less than the initiative for the conquest of Egypt by the Fāṭimids.

Mu'izz, it is true, had long included the conquest of Egypt in his political and strategical programme, and the first preparations for the invasion had been made as early as 967. The moment at which to strike had not, however, been determined; and the sources show that the two immediate factors fixing it were (*a*) the death of Kāfūr and (*b*) Ya'qūb b. Killis's coming to al-Mu'izz.

Both events occurred in the same year (968) and stand in a causal relationship to one another. That the death of Kāfūr precipitated al-Mu'izz's decision to advance is asserted by Ibn Khallikān.[3] But, on the other hand, Ibn Taghribirdi, as we have just seen, ascribes considerable importance to the factor of Ya'qūb's presence at the 'Ubaydite court. It may be supposed that the personal knowledge of conditions in Egypt which he had acquired under Kāfūr, his information on the weakness of the Government, the unreliability of the troops, the financial crises, crop failures, epidemics, famines, and all

Jauhar *en route* and returned at once with him in order to assist in the conquest of Egypt. But others report that Ya'qūb b. Killis proceeded on his way to Maghrib. The former account is entirely precluded by the fact that Jauhar did not set out on his Egyptian campaign before 969, whereas Ya'qūb b. Killis had already arrived in Maghrib by 968.

[1] *Ibn aṣ-Ṣairafi*, p. 92; cf. *Ibn Khallikān*, ii, 444; *adh-Dhahabi*, i, 180.

[2] *Ibn Taghribirdi*, ed. Juynboll, ii, 396: فهرب يعقوب بن كلّس ... الى المغرب وهو احد اكبر اسباب حركة المعزّ وارسال جوهر القاعد الى الديار المصرية.

[3] *Ibn Khall.*, ii, 134: "When the news of Kāfūr's death reached al-Mu'izz . . . al-Mu'izz notified Jauhar to prepare to leave for Egypt."

the other factors favouring such a campaign, spurred al-Mu'izz on, and we may safely subscribe to Lane-Poole's cautious conclusion that "His (Ya'qūb's) representations confirmed the Fāṭimid Caliph's resolve".[1]

An account of the Egyptian campaign would be out of place here. Ya'qūb b. Killis had no share in its strategy. He was then an administrative official, an authority in the field of economics; it was only after Egypt had been conquered and conditions stabilized there that he returned to Cairo and reappeared in history.

Whilst Jauhar, after successfully invading Egypt, was striving to re-establish order there, so as to hand the country over to his master in a tranquil and prosperous condition,[2] the latter remained in Maghrib and Ya'qūb b. Killis stayed with him. There is no doubt that he spent the years 968 to 973 in Maghrib and did not proceed to Egypt until the latter date, together with al-Mu'izz. On this point the sources are unanimous. According to Maqrīzi, Ya'qūb b. Killis remained in the service of al-Mu'izz without interruption "until he went forth from Maghrib to Egypt in the year 362/972–3".[3]

Taxation and Monetary Reform

Thus, after an absence of five years, Egypt again became in 973 the scene of Ya'qūb b. Killis's activity; but now under a new master. "Upon arriving in Egypt," says Yaḥyā b. Sa'īd,[4] "al-Mu'izz placed him in charge of Egypt's ground taxes," and adds that Ya'qūb continued to occupy this office until his appointment to the vizierate by al-'Azīz. His duties, however, were not confined to the ground tax; in actual fact he had to reorganize the entire administration of taxation and finance. In Ibn Muyassar [5] we read :—

[1] Lane-Poole, *History of Egypt*, p. 101.

[2] Cf. Maqrīzi, *Itti'āẓ*, pp. 76 ff.; *Khiṭaṭ*, ii, 226.

[3] *Maqrīzi*, ii, 5; *Ibn Khallikān*, ii, 443; *adh-Dhahabi*, i, 180.

[4] Ed. Kratch., p. 443; ed. Cheikho, p. 172.

[5] *Ibn Muyassar*, pp. 45 ff.; *Maqrīzi*, ii, 6, parallel version with slight changes; also in *Itti'āẓ*, ed. Bunz, pp. 95 ff.

"In the year 973 al-Mu'izz appointed Ya'qūb b. Killis and 'Aslūj b. Ḥasan [1] administrators of the ground tax and every branch of revenue such as market dues and harbour tolls, tithes, poll-taxes, endowments, inheritance taxes (i.e. death duties), police, and everything connected therewith, both in Egypt and in the other provinces of the Fāṭimid Empire."

Ya'qūb b. Killis and his colleague thus became, in effect, the heads of the entire financial administration and the most influential persons in al-Mu'izz's entourage.[2]

In connection with the administration of revenue Ya'qūb b. Killis found himself faced with the need for a *monetary reform*. The references scattered in the sources enable us to recognize the following main features of this reform. In 969 Jauhar had already endeavoured to bring some order into the undermined and chaotic currency system of Egypt.[3] He reopened the mint (*dār aḍ-ḍarb*) and had a new dīnār [4] struck in the name of al-Mu'izz.[5]

This Mu'izzi dīnār, as it was called, and the Rāḍi dīnār [6] previously current, had to be brought into a new relation to the silver coin, the dirham. In the year 970, therefore, Jauhar issued an ordinance fixing the ratio of the Rāḍi dīnār to the dirham at $25\frac{1}{2}$. But, as the sources tell us, people did not observe these provisions. Further currency measures taken by Jauhar

[1] This official is only mentioned together with Ya'qūb b. Killis.

[2] The sources further relate that al-Mu'izz provided Ya'qūb b. Killis and 'Aslūj b. Ḥasan with a decree, which was read out on a Friday from the Minbar of the Ṭūlūnid Mosque, to the effect that the powers of the previous tax-farmers were to be restricted and that these two officials, sitting in the Emirate Building, were to be applied to in all matters connected with the leasing and assessment of landed property, the payment of arrears, complaints, etc.

[3] *Itti'āẓ*, pp. 76, 80.

[4] Cf. Lane-Poole, *Catalogue of Oriental Coins in the British Museum*, vol. iv, No. 29, pl. i.

[5] See Maqrīzi, *Shudhūr*, ed. L. A. Mayer, part i, p. 11, l. 12 ff.

[6] Named after the 'Abbāsid Caliph ar-Rāḍi (934–940). According to *Muqaddasi*, i, 204, this Rāḍi dīnār was especially current in Egypt. Cf. *Journ. Asiat.*, 1879, p. 503; 1880, p. 244.

in succeeding years, and related by Maqrīzi,[1] proved ineffectual. We even hear of a tumult of a group of bankers or money-changers in Cairo, which ensued in 973 as a result of his new measures. It would seem that Jewish money-changers of Cairo also played a part in it.[2]

Ya'qūb b. Killis and 'Aslūj b. Ḥasan were far more successful in this regard. Their reform, of which many parallel accounts exist, consisted in accepting none but Mu'izzi dīnārs in payment at the revenue offices.[3] The object of this measure was no doubt to stabilize the Mu'izzi dīnār for the purpose of increasing the state revenues. At the same time it necessarily resulted in a slump of the Rāḍi dīnār, which is said to have depreciated by one-third of its value. The value of the stabilized Mu'izzi dīnār was henceforth 15½ dīnārs.[4]

This reform resulted in great losses for the common people, it is true, but it was in the interest of the state and of sound financial administration. The reason why increased revenues were so necessary is as follows: al-Mu'izz had spent his entire fortune upon the Egyptian campaign,[5] but had hoped to find stored-up treasures in the conquered territory with which to recoup himself. Being disappointed in this expectation the Fāṭimid administration had to look about for other sources of money, and the currency reform, we are explicitly told, was designed to fill the exchequer "in order to cover the vast amounts spent by al-Mu'izz upon Egypt."

The sources cannot praise too highly the success of this method of procuring funds. Enormous sums are said to have

[1] *Maqrīzi*, ii, 6; cf. *Itti'āẓ*, p. 80, 9–12; 87, 11 ff.

[2] The name of the market official who had to interfere was Sulaymān b. 'Ushara. He punished some of the money-changers and decreed that Jews must wear special badges; cf. *Itti'āẓ*, 78.

[3] *Ibn Muyassar*, p. 45; Maqrīzi, *Itti'āẓ*, 97.

[4] According to Maqrīzi, *Shudhūr*, p. 11, l. 19 ff., the depreciation was more than a quarter of value.

[5] An official of the treasury, wishing to convey an idea of the cost of the expedition, tells how the troops entering Fusṭāṭ included two camels, each laden with two boxes of empty money-bags. Their contents had been eaten up by the supplies and wages of the troops.

found their way into the state exchequer. In a single day the income from Fusṭāṭ alone was 50,000, sometimes even 120,000, Mu'izzi dīnārs, and from Damietta and Ushmūnayn more than 200,000 dīnārs were received in one day. The authors are quite astonished, and can only say: "Nothing like it has ever been heard of in the country." [1]

Thanks to this success, Ya'qūb b. Killis was accorded a sort of monopoly in the administration, and was now permitted to direct the affairs of al-Mu'izz with unlimited powers.[2]

The success of the monetary reform, and of the financial administration generally, will always be associated with the name of Ya'qūb b. Killis in the history of Egypt. It was he who laid the foundations of a sound and efficient financial administration, upon which al-Mu'izz's successors were able to build. Viewed in the light of this success, C. H. Becker [3] was justified in calling him "a financial genius and organizer of the first order", and in declaring that "the internal administration of the Fāṭimid Empire was created by him".

2. As Vizier under al-'Azīz

After the death of al-Mu'izz and upon the accession of his son al-'Azīz in 976, Ya'qūb b. Killis's position in the Government was more than confirmed; his functions as Inspector and Minister of Taxation and Finance were even enlarged by the placing of "other affairs" under his control.[4]

The nature of these other affairs is not specified. We learn for the first time in this connection, however, that Ya'qūb b. Killis was also consulted on matters of foreign policy and strategy.[5] This advisory function regarding foreign affairs is significant, as it contributed to his further advancement and to his attainment of the highest dignity in the Fāṭimid Empire, the vizierate.

[1] *Ibn Muyassar*, 46; cf. Maqrīzi, *Itti'āẓ*, p. 97.
[2] *Maqrīzi*, ii, 6.
[3] *Enc. Isl.*, s.v. Egypt.
[4] *Maqrīzi*, ii, 6.
[5] *Ibn al-Athīr*, viii, 484.

His appointment as vizier was connected with Jauhar's unsuccessful expedition of 365/975 against the rebel Aftekīn of Damascus. Jauhar had been compelled to retreat first from Damascus and then from Ascalon, where he had entrenched himself, and to sign an armistice by which he ceded the entire territory from Ascalon northward to Aftekīn. Al-'Azīz was very angry at this and, it would seem, dismissed Jauhar from office upon his return to Cairo in 977. And now al-'Azīz fell back entirely upon the counsel of Ya'qūb b. Killis, who advised an expedition against Aftekīn. Al-'Azīz thereupon took the field himself and returned victorious with Aftekīn as prisoner. We hear that one of the first acts after his return was to appoint Ya'qūb b. Killis vizier.[1]

The fact of Ya'qūb b. Killis's appointment to the vizierate is recorded in all the sources. Regarding the date, however, there are divergent statements. These discrepancies, however, are mainly due to the confusion of two stages in his appointment to the vizierate : (*a*) his appointment to the office of vizier in 367/977, and (*b*) his acquisition of the title of الوزير الاجلّ in 368/978.[2]

The significance of Ya'qūb's appointment is heightened by the circumstance that it was the first appointment of a vizier by a Fāṭimid ruler in Egypt. The sources lay particular stress on this fact, saying that he was اول من وزر للدولة الفاطمية فى الديار المصرية.[3]

Of his activities as vizier we mention only two important points : (*a*) the organization of the administration into several

[1] *Yaḥyā b. Sa'īd*, ed. Kratchk., vol. xxiii, p. 391. The edition of Cheikho contains no reference to this point.

[2] al-'Azīz ordered further that letters and audiences should reach him only through the medium of Ya'qūb b. Killis, whose name was to be set on every official document. Besides *Yaḥyā b. Sa'īd*, ed. Kratchk., xxiii, p. 392, cf. *Ibn Khallikān*, p. 442, 13 ; *Maqrīzi*, ii, 6 ; ii, 226 ; ii, 284.

[3] *Maqrīzi*, ii, 6 ; *Ibn Khallikān*, ii, 440 ; *as-Suyūti*, ii, 152. Some sources refer to him as the Vizier under al-Mu'izz—so *Ibn Abī Uṣaibi'a*, ii, 87 ; *Ibn al-Qifti*, 106, 8 ; *Histoire d'Abraham le Syrien*, p. 382 ; Maqrīzi, *Itti'āẓ*, 95, 2. According to *Maqr.*, i, 352 and 377, Jauhar was already the bearer of the title vizier ; but this is incorrect.

dīwāns.[1] Each dīwān was equipped with a definite number of *kuttāb*, and in the case of the *dīwān al-amwāl* also with a number of *jahābidha*. These offices were located in the palace of Ya'qūb b. Killis,[2] and worked under the inspection of a special *zimām*[3]; (*b*) the institution of storehouses, a characteristic feature of the inner administration of the Fāṭimids. He is stated to have fitted out many خزانة, which were likewise housed in his palace, each being controlled by a special *nāẓir*.

Thus he administered the whole of the Fāṭimid domains, which at that time included, besides Egypt, Syria, and Maghrib, the holy cities of Mecca and Medīna.[4] All officials in these lands and all the affairs of the realm were subordinated to him.[5]

Temporary Fall and Reappointment

" In the year 983–4," we read,[6] " al-'Azīz ordered his vizier Ya'qūb b. Killis to be arrested, . . . confiscated all his property, and removed 200,000 dīnārs from the house of the vizier to the treasury of the Palace." [6] Without any reasons given we read further that Ya'qūb b. Killis was incarcerated in the citadel and the administration entrusted to Khabir b. al-Qāsim.[7] What was the reason of this sudden dismissal ?

It is in Ibn al-Athīr and Ibn Taghribirdi[8] that the context betrays the cause of this fall from grace as being connected with

[1] *Maqr.*, ii, 6 ; cf. *Maqr.*, ii, 226. A special treatment of each of these dīwāns and its purpose would exceed the limits of this study.

[2] This palace was called الوزيرية ; cf. *Yaḥyā b. Sa'īd*, ed. Cheikho, p. 144 ; ed. Kratchk., xviii, p. 414.

[3] I venture to emendate زمان into زمام in *Maqr.*, ii, 6, which is a frequently mentioned expression in the fiscal administration.

[4] *Maqr.*, ii, 6.

[5] Cf. *al-Kindi : Governors of Egypt*, pp. 590, 591, 593.

[6] *Yaḥyā b. Sa'īd*, ed. Cheikho, p. 164 ; ed. Kratchk., xxiii, p. 433 ; *Ibn aṣ-Ṣairafi*, p. 94 ; *Ibn Khallikān*, ii, 442 ; *Maqr.*, ii, 6.

[7] *Ibn aṣ-Ṣairafi*, 90, devotes a detailed biography to this Khabir b. al-Qāsim. He was the first successor of Ya'qūb b. Killis to the vizierate.

[8] *Ibn al-Athīr*, viii, 487 ; *Ibn Taghribirdi*, ed. Popper, ii, 23.

Aftekīn, the erstwhile rebel of Syria. We have related how al-ʿAzīz brought him back captive. Contrary to expectation, this deadly enemy of the Fāṭimids was not only pardoned but was loaded with honours and even given a position at Court. Henceforth he belonged to al-ʿAzīz's retinue. Yaʿqūb b. Killis strongly disapproved of this treatment, and, after years full of rivalry between the two, finally Yaʿqūb b. Killis had his enemy poisoned. al-ʿAzīz was very angry and, suspecting the vizier of the deed, imprisoned him.

All the sources are agreed, however, that Yaʿqūb's imprisonment lasted less than two months. After that al-ʿAzīz not only restored to Yaʿqūb b. Killis all his confiscated property, but added rich gifts and new honours.[1] A document signed by the Caliph proclaimed his reinstatement in the administration of the government,[2] and henceforth Ibn Killis "continued to conduct the affairs of al-ʿAzīz without interruption until his death in the year 380/991".[3]

Why was he reinstated so quickly after his arrest?

"*Following the dismissal of the vizier the business of al-ʿAzīz's Government came to a standstill. He therefore formally summoned him and bestowed the vizierate upon him anew.*"[4]

Death

If the temporary dismissal of Yaʿqūb b. Killis in 983 was sufficient to create such a sad loss, his death in 380/991, after serving al-ʿAzīz for more than twelve years, brought home with a vengeance his vital importance to Egypt. It

[1] *Yaḥyā b. Saʿīd*, ed. Cheikho, 164; ed. Kratchk., p. 433; *Ibn Khallikān*, ii, 443; *Ibn Ṣairafi*, p. 94; *Maqr.*, ii, p. 6, and others specify among other things a bodyguard of 1,500 men for his person. Cf. also *Ibn al-Athīr*, viii, 487.

[2] *Maqr.*, ii, 6.

[3] *Ibn Khall.*, ii, 441; *Maqrīzi*, ii, 6; cf. *Ibn Taghr.*, ed. Popper, ii, 45.

[4] *Ibn al-Athīr*, viii, 487: ثم وقفت امور دولة ا عزيز باعتزال الوزير فخلع عليه واعاده الى وزارته. An interesting parallel to this testimony regarding the indispensability of Yaʿqūb b. Killis is offered by the passage quoted above from at-Tanūkhi concerning the two Jewish Court bankers of al-Muqtadir; cf. above, p. 28.

would go beyond the limits of this study to quote in full the reports of the sources regarding his sickness and death. The mourning of the Caliph and all Egypt on his account clearly shows once more his value to the Fāṭimid dynasty of Egypt.

In the history of Islam there are few parallels for such a deep personal contact between Caliph and Vizier, master and servant. One of the sources rightly remarks: "The fact that he was leaving the world did not prevent him from giving wise advice to his master and displaying affection towards him, which is the way of faithful friends." [1]

Indeed, C. H. Becker [2] is right in saying of Ya'qūb b. Killis that the Fāṭimid government could find no more capable and expert administrator of the country's economic policy and that the great prosperity of the Nile Valley under the Fāṭimids is associated with his name.

Jewish Officials under Ya'qūb b. Killis

In the days of al-'Azīz the Fāṭimid Empire extended as far as Syria and Palestine. Among the huge army of officials required for the administration of the Empire various Jewish officials are found acting, especially in Syria, in co-operation

[1] As he lay on his death-bed he was visited by the Caliph, who, knowing his almost hopeless condition, addressed him thus: "O Ya'qūb, how I wish you were for sale so that I might buy you with my kingdom, or that you could be ransomed and I might ransom you. Is there any desire that you wish me to fulfil?" Ya'qūb wept and kissed his hand, which he placed upon his eyes. He then said: "O Prince of the Faithful, I have no personal desire. . . . But what I would say with regard to the concerns of your Empire is this: Keep the peace with the Byzantines so long as they maintain it; be satisfied with recognition in public prayer and coinage on the part of the Ḥamdānids; spare not Mufarrij b. Daghfal b. Jarrāḥ if ever you get him into your power." *Ibn al-Qalānisi*, 32; *Maqr.*, ii, 7; *Ecl.*, iii, 185. Al-'Azīz was present at the funeral, said the prayer over him, and laid him with his own hand in the grave. He went home sorrowful at his loss and had the public offices closed for some days afterwards. According to Maqrīzi, al-'Azīz ate nothing at all that day, nor did he invite any guests to join him. As a sign of mourning he also rode without any sunshade.

[2] *Enc. Isl.*, ii, 398.

with Ya'qūb b. Killis. These Jewish officials deserve a place in our study.

Though Ya'qūb b. Killis had given up his Judaism, he remained in touch with Jews even after his conversion. In Maghrib, as we have already learnt, he had at once joined the Jews at the Court of al-Mu'izz, remaining a member of their group until he returned to Egypt.[1] Under al-Mu'izz in Egypt he had a Jewish friend named Mūsā and when, we are informed by a Christian source, his Jewish friend was once insulted by a bishop at a religious disputation, Ya'qūb took the part of the Jew and rebuked the Christian.[2]

His attitude towards Jews is further illustrated by their employment in responsible posts in the Syrian administration.[3]

Thus we learn of a certain ابن ابى العود Ibn Abi'l-'Ūd al-yahūdi from Ibn al-Qalānisi, and up to the present from him alone.[4] Ibn al-Qalānisi informs us that this Jew was a representative of Ya'qūb b. Killis, supervising the latter's affairs and property and keeping him informed of internal developments in Syria (اخبار البلد). It seems that together with this business relationship he was also employed by the

[1] *Ibn Qalānisi,* p. 33; cf. *Ibn Khallikān,* ii, 443, 5.

[2] *Histoire d'Abraham le Syrien,* ed. Leroy, 1909, pp. 380–400; 1910, pp. 26–41.

[3] *Ibn Khallikān,* ii, 443, also leaves room for the view that Ya'qūb b. Killis died a Jew مات على دينه and professed Islam only outwardly. But, on the other hand, he reports that he spoke slightingly of Judaism and the Jewish religion. It must be said, however, that Ibn Killis had a great affection for Islamic science and literature, and supported scholars, poets, theologians, jurists, grammarians, reciters of the Qur'ān, etc., on a large scale, holding learned assemblies weekly at his palace which were frequented by the "society" of Cairo. Many of the scholars he supported and rewarded dedicated books to their Mæcenas, while poems were also written in his honour (*Ibn Abī Uṣaibi'a,* i, 247; ii, 87–9; *Ibn al-Qifṭi,* 106, 8 and 285). He himself wrote a book on Islamic law كتاب الفقه, which was known as الرسالة الوزيرية. It was dedicated to al-'Azīz, who is said to have made it the basis of legal decisions. *Ibn aṣ-Ṣairafi,* p. 21; *Yaḥyā b. Sa'īd,* ed. Kratch., p. 433; ed. Cheikho, p. 172; *Ibn Khallikān,* ii, 441; *Maqrīzi,* ii, 6–7.

[4] *Ibn al-Qalānisi,* p. 29.

Vizier in a political capacity. Bakjūr, the Governor of Syria, regarded him as Ya'qūb b. Killis's secret agent and hence an undesirable onlooker; so he had Ibn Abi'l-'Ūd slain in the year 372/982. When Ya'qūb b. Killis heard of this action he was furious and reported the matter to the Caliph al-'Azīz, claiming that this step on the part of the Governor meant the commencement of a revolution against the state.

A few years later we hear once again, from Ibn al-Qalānisi, of a Jew named Ibn Abi'l-'Ūd, with the added epithet الصغير, i.e. the younger. This Ibn Abi'l-'Ūd junior was probably a brother or son of the other one, who had been entrusted with the affairs of Ya'qūb b. Killis after his kinsman had been slain. From Ibn al-Qalānisi we learn that he was put in charge of the finances of the Vizier, and hence held a post in the financial administration of Syria. It is expressly stated of him that he retained a high and assured position in the service of al-'Azīz.[1]

While these two Jewish officials could not hitherto be identified from Hebrew sources, another Jewish colleague of Ya'qūb b. Killis in the administration of Syria, one Manasha b. Ibrāhīm, is known from Hebrew Geniza fragments.

The name of this official is variously given by different authorities. Ibn al-Athīr[2] calls him simply Manashā the Jew منشا اليهودى; Ibn aṣ-Ṣairafi[3] speaks of him as Manashā b. Ibrāhīm; Ibn al-Qalānisi[4] knows him as Manashā b. al-Farrār al-yahūdi; while we find his full name recorded in the form Manashā b. Ibrāhīm b. al-Farrār al-yahūdi.[5] In the Hebrew Geniza fragments J. Mann reads القزاز instead of الفرار.[6]

This Manashā b. Ibrāhīm first appears in the sources in the year 980 as one engaged in administering Ya'qūb b. Killis's

[1] Loc. cit., p. 40.

[2] *Ibn al-Athīr*, ix, pp. 20, 54, 81–2; *Ibn Taghrib.*, ed. Popper, p. 4; *Ibn Iyās*, i, 47–8.

[3] p. 88.

[4] Op. cit., p. 25.

[5] *Ibn al-Qalānisi*, p. 33; *Eclipse*, iii, 186.

[6] Mann, *Jews*, i, p. 20; ii, 16, 153.

property. According to Ibn al-Qalānisi he was appointed على العسكر, and is described as Kātib al-Jaish, Secretary to the Army Office. He must have played a leading part in the military administration of Syria, as all orders from the Caliph al-ʻAzīz or his Vizier Yaʻqūb b. Killis, when transmitted to the then Governor of Syria, Baltakīn, were also addressed to him as the closest collaborator of the Governor. From Yaʻqūb b. Killis Manashā used to receive instructions regarding the conduct of civil and military affairs in Syria.[1] In spite of all intrigues, revolts, and conspiracies of the Syrian officials, he always kept his faith with al-ʻAzīz and his Vizier, with whom he was obviously connected for years by a link of trust.

He appears in the sources again after the death of Yaʻqūb b. Killis, when a Coptic Christian, ʻĪsā b. Nesṭorius, was appointed Vizier by al-ʻAzīz. Manashā must have rendered important services to the Fāṭimid administration in Syria, for he was appointed (990) the representative of the new Vizier and governor in Syria.[2]

Of his activities as governor the sources report no more than his one-sided policy regarding Government personnel. Thus we are told : " ʻĪsā b. Nesṭorius was a Christian. He administered affairs, amassed money and favoured the Christians, whom he placed in office to the exclusion of the Muslim clerks and officials. In Syria he appointed as his deputy a Jew named Manashā b. Ibrāhīm b. al-Farrār, who dealt with the Jews as ʻĪsā dealt with the Christians ; so that the followers of these two religions came into occupation of all the offices." [2]

The opposition resulting from this one-sided policy regarding personnel led to his speedy dismissal by the Caliph. The sources [3] report that one of the Muslims drew up a complaint

[1] *Ibn al-Qalānisi*, pp. 25, 29–30, 33, 40.

[2] *Ibn Iyās*, i, 48–9.

[3] *Ibn al-Athīr*, ix, 20, 54 ; *Ibn al-Qalānisi*, pp. 28–33 ; *Eclipse*, iii, 185. These sources show obviously a tendency against the *ahl adh-Dhimma*.

which he gave to a woman, whom he induced by the offer of a large sum to place herself in the way of the ruler of Egypt, al-'Azīz, and put the complaint into his hand. The contents were: "Your Majesty, by him who has exalted the Christians through 'Īsā b. Nesṭorius and the Jews through Manashā b. al-Farrār and has humiliated the Muslims through you—I pray you to examine my case. . . ." The Caliph read the complaint and took counsel with his Qāḍi Ibn Nu'mān, who held the complaint to be justified. Thereupon al-'Azīz "ordered the arrest of Ibn Nesṭorius and all the Christian clerks, and wrote to Syria ordering the arrest of Manashā b. al-Farrār and all the Jewish officials.[1] He commanded that the offices and public posts should be restored to Muslim clerks and that the Qāḍi should be appointed to oversee them throughout the Empire." [2]

This meant the end of Manashā's public career. We hear nothing more of him. By 991 there was already a Muslim governor of Syria in his place.[2] One of his sons, named 'Ādiyā, seems to have been in Government service, as we learn from the Hebrew Geniza fragments.[3]

3. Ya'qūb b. Killis and the Jewish Sources

In his *Mediaeval Jewish Chronicles* Adolf Neubauer [4] published a Hebrew chronicle, ספר היוחסין, in which the author, a certain Aḥima'az b. Palṭīēl of Southern Italy, records in rhymed prose the outstanding personalities of his family and the adventures that befell them between the years

[1] There must have been other Jews and Christians in the service of Ya'qūb b. Killis, as can be inferred from the dissatisfaction of the populace which expressed itself in satirical verses against the Vizier. Cf. Bar Hebræus, *Mukhtaṣar*, Beyruth, 1890, p. 310; *Ibn al-Athīr*, ix, 82; *Ibn Taghr.*, ed. Popper, pp. 4 ff.; *Ibn Iyās*, i, 48.

[2] *Ibn aṣ-Ṣairafi*, p. 88, 3. 'Īsā b. Nesṭorius was reappointed Vizier, but had to undertake to employ only Muslims in government offices.

[3] Mann, *The Jews in Egypt*, ii, 11–13. Ibid., Additions in *Hebrew Union College Annual*, iii, p. 257.

[4] ii, Oxford, 1895, pp. 111–132. Another edition with an English translation has been published by M. Salzmann, *The Chronicle of Aḥima'az*, New York, 1924.

850–1054, for the benefit of posterity. In this family chronicle one of the outstanding figures is a certain Rabbi Palṭīēl b. Shefaṭia, who, it is reported, won the confidence of the Fāṭimid ruler al-Mu'izz by his astrological knowledge when the latter's troops were besieging Oria in Southern Italy. Al-Mu'izz made him counsellor and Vizier of his kingdom in Maghrib (Kairuwān) and later at Cairo. In this capacity he also served the following Caliph, al-'Azīz. The chronicle of Aḥima'az deals in detail [2] with the wondrous rise of this Rabbi Palṭīēl, relating the considerable part he played in the conquest of Egypt and the establishment of the Fāṭimid Empire, and says of him: "Further details regarding the deeds of Palṭiel, how the King set him in charge of all his treasures and gave him the control of the Kingdom of Egypt and the Kingdom of the Syrians as far as Mesopotamia and over the Land of Israel unto Jerusalem, as also of his ruling, his power, and his wealth whereby the King raised him on high and distinguished him, are written in the books of the history of the Egyptian Kingdom." [1]

That such a figure as Rabbi Palṭīēl, who, according to the chronicle, must have played so considerable a part in the public life of the Fāṭimid period, should be mentioned in the Arabic sources of that period must naturally be expected. This expectation, however, is not fulfilled. None of the numerous Arabic works on the Fāṭimid period mention any Palṭīēl. Considering the friendly attitude of the Fāṭimids towards the Jews, the reticence of the sources regarding Palṭīēl can hardly be attributed to his religion. For this reason it has been asked whether the whole tale of Rabbi Palṭīēl is no more than a pure invention, or whether Palṭīēl is perhaps known to the Arab historians under some other name.

This question engaged the attention of no less a scholar than *de Goeje*. He considered Palṭīēl to be a historic personality, and agreed with *D. Kaufmann* that "there can be no doubt

[1] Ed. Neubauer, ii, p. 129.

of a historical element in the story reported by Aḥima'az, despite the legendary garb in which it is arrayed ".[1]

Under what name, then, does Palṭīēl appear in Arabic sources? De Goeje says: "I knew, however, of only one person whose story in general corresponds with that of Palṭīēl, namely General Jauhar, the conqueror of Egypt and founder of Cairo." On the basis of details of Jauhar's life as reported by the Arabic sources, de Goeje attempts to prove his identity with the Palṭīēl of the chronicle, reaching the conclusion that "everything that Aḥima'az tells of Palṭīēl's share in the conquest of Egypt corresponds precisely to what the Arab historians have to tell of Jauhar ".[2]

This proposed solution by de Goeje has also been supported by *A. Marx*, who, in the light of a Hebrew fragment, regards "the identification of Palṭīēl and Jauhar as probable in the highest degree ".[3]

Nonetheless, there are considerations which militate against the proposed identification. It has already been admitted that the difference in names does not represent an insurmountable difficulty.[4] But in our opinion there is one element with which the person to be identified as the Palṭīēl of the chronicle must in any case comply: he must be a Jew or of Jewish origin. In an attempt at identification, numerous details of his rise, his influence, even the difference in names, might well be overlooked; the fact of his being a Jew or of Jewish origin, however, is an essential part of his character and personality.[5] As Jauhar, however, is never referred to as a

[1] D. Kaufmann, Beiträge zur Geschichte Ägyptens aus jüdischen Quellen, *ZDMG.*, li, p. 436. Cf. also *MGWJ.*, vol. xl, p. 530.

[2] de Goeje, Djauhar=Palṭīēl, *ZDMG.*, lii, p. 75.

[3] A. Marx, Studies in Gaonic History and Literature, *JQR.*, 1910, vol. i, pp. 78–85.

[4] de Goeje, loc. cit.

[5] By regarding Palṭīēl as an Egyptian Nagīd, Poznanski (*REJ.*, xlviii, p. 145), Gottheil (*Jew. Encycl.*, v, 61, 68), and Kaufmann (*ZDMG.*, li, p. 436) show that they realize how essential the Jewish factor in him was. Cf. also B. Dinaburg in *Zion*, ed. Jerusalem, 1929, vol. iii, pp. 64–5.

Jew or as of Jewish origin, we do not see our way to agree with the view generally held.

When we examine the Arabic sources regarding the period of al-Mu'izz and al-'Azīz, we find indeed only one man of known Jewish origin whose political influence, importance, and rise at the court show in their main lines much similarity to those of Palṭīēl. He is the Vizier Ya'qūb b. Killis.

It is a surprising fact that Jewish sources know nothing of Ya'qūb b. Killis, whose rôle has been described above. The shortage of Hebrew sources may be responsible for this, and possibly his conversion to Islam, as the result of which Jewish sources might prefer to ignore him, though, as we have seen, he maintained friendly relations with Jews after his conversion as well.

Be this as it may, should there not be some sort of connection between Ya'qūb b. Killis and Palṭīēl? The asking of such a question immediately raises difficulties as great as those met in the case of the Jauhar–Palṭīēl identification. We hear nothing of any astrological knowledge on the part of Ya'qūb b. Killis; he comes from Baghdād and not from Southern Italy; and there are many other discrepancies. But in view of the legendary character of the chronicle, too much weight does not need to be attached to details. On the other hand, Ya'qūb b. Killis satisfies some of the most important criteria by which any identification with Palṭīēl can be and should be tested: he was of Jewish extraction, was appointed adviser by al-Mu'izz and al-'Azīz, with whom he was on friendly terms, participated in the conquest of Egypt and in the foundation of the new state, and finally has his activities reported in the Arabic chronicles.

D. Kaufmann suggested the possibility of Ya'qūb b. Killis and Palṭīēl being identical, but discredited it on the grounds that "any identification of the two is unthinkable . . . because Ya'qūb b. Killis was a convert to Islam". This, however, is no decisive factor; otherwise the identification with Jauhar, who was not even of Jewish origin, is even more unlikely. Actually the Hebrew fragment published by Marx in support of the Palṭīēl–Jauhar identification provides good evidence that there was a connection between Palṭīēl and Ya'qūb b. Killis. This fragment refers *inter alia* to a son of Palṭīēl named Ya'qūb, of whom Marx himself says[1]: " I identify without hesitation Jacob the *son* of Palṭīēl with the Vizier Ya'qūb b. Killis. . . ." If so, the suggestion of any connection between Jauhar and Palṭīēl falls flat, while increasing the likelihood of a Palṭīēl–Ya'qūb b. Killis relation still more. No final and definite opinion, however, can yet be expressed.

II. THE BANŪ SAHL OF TUSTAR

1.

No mediaeval Islamic dynasty so facilitated the participation of the *ahl adh-Dhimma* in public, economic, and political affairs as did the Fāṭimid rulers of Egypt. Disregarding transitory phenomena such as the reactionary fanaticism of the Caliph al-Ḥākim, the reign of the Fāṭimids was, taken all in all, a golden age for Jews and Christians, and one in which their qualities and capacities could be devoted to the service of the State without hindrance.

The previous section showed the close co-operation of Jews in the new State under al-Mu'izz and al-'Azīz. This policy of tolerance was kept up by the Caliphs aẓ-Ẓāhir and al-Mustanṣir ; thanks to it Jews are again found occupying prominent positions in the State service and in economic life during the first half of the eleventh century.

Sources dealing with this period refer primarily to two Jews, in immediate contact with the Court, who maintained a commercial and banking house. They are the Banū Sahl, Abū Sa'd Ibrāhīm b. Sahl at-Tustari and Abū Naṣr Aaron b. Sahl at-Tustari. The outstanding position in Fāṭimid State life filled by these two Jews, their rôle and their influence,

[1] Studies, *JQR.*, 1910, p. 84.

has, however, not yet been the subject of a special study. To provide this, on the basis of all available sources, is the intention of the following section.

Names

The names of the two brothers,[1] especially that of Abū Sa'd, are not always given uniformly in the sources. Maqrīzi calls him Abū Sa'd Ibrāhīm b. Sahl,[2] and also Abū Sa'd Sahl b. Aaron,[3] which is probably a confusion. Neither is there any consistency at all with regard to the Kunya Abū Sa'd. Nāṣir-i-Khosrau [4] writes Abū Sa'īd, a form also found in the manuscript of Ibn aṣ-Ṣairafi [5] and other sources.[6] It may be regarded as certain, however, that Ibrāhīm's Kunya was Abū Sa'd (ابو سعد), for this form is plainly legible in the Hebrew Geniza documents that have been preserved.[7]

As a rule the names of the brothers are followed by the nisbe " the Jew ", *al-Yahūdi*, and there is no doubt that they were actually Jews.[8]

In addition to that nisbe the names of Abū Sa'd and Abū Naṣr are almost invariably accompanied by the expression *at-Tustari* " of Tustar ", the town in Southern Persia. They were therefore Persian Jews, who either came from Tustar themselves or were descended from those who came thence.

Until well into the first third of the tenth century Tustar was an important economic centre, in the prosperity of which, as Miskawaih [9] notes, Jews had a large share. The reason

1 ابو سعد ابراهيم بن سهل التسترى.
ابو نصر هرون بن سهل التسترى.

2 *Maqrīzi*, i, 424.

3 *Maqrīzi*, i, 355.

4 *Sefer Nāmeh*, pp. 55–6.

5 *Ibn aṣ-Ṣairafi*, p. 73, n. 5 ; corrected by the editor in ابو سعد.

6 *Ibn al-Athīr*, x, 55 ; *Ibn Taghrib.*, ii, 183 ; *Ṣubḥ al-A'shā*, iii, 489.

7 J. Mann, *The Jews in Egypt and Palestine*, i, 76 ff. ; ii, 75 ff. ; id., *Texts and Studies*, pp. 371–385 ; Gottheil-Worrell, *Geniza-Fragments*, pp. 143, 147. Cf. also *Ibn Muyassar*, 6, 8 ; also *Maqrīzi*, i, 355, 424.

8 From Yāqūt, *Mu'jam*, iv, 1045, 11, we learn that the nisbe *al-yahūdi* is not always conclusive.

9 *Misk.*, i, 357.

for the migration of the Banū Sahl or their forefathers was probably the persecutions to which the Jews of Tustar and its vicinity were subjected in the days of the Buwayhids.[1] They may not have proceeded direct to Fusṭāṭ. We know that in Baghdād there was a quarter inhabited by people from Tustar,[2] and this may have been a station in their wanderings. The rise of a new economic centre in Egypt and the transfer of the political and economic hegemony from Baghdād to Fusṭāṭ owing to the supremacy of the Fāṭimid dynasty no doubt determined their ultimate goal.[3]

In Cairo these Persian Jews would have settled in the Jewish quarter. At that time there was already a considerable Jewish population in Cairo which, as we know from the Geniza, consisted of a number of communities divided according to their geographical origin: that of the Byzantines, the Damascenes, the Baghdādis, etc. The family of the Banū Sahl probably joined the already existent Babylonian-'Irāqi community,[4] within which they developed their economic activity.

Inner Organization

Just as in the Baghdād firm of Joseph, Aaron and Co. we recognized an enterprise based upon blood relationship, so here we find the brothers Abū Sa'd and Abū Naṣr constituting the single firm of Sahl Brothers. Maqrīzi describes them explicitly as "two Jewish Brothers",[5] and as such they are also mentioned in other sources. The Geniza material in particular has a good deal to say about them both. The Arabic sources speak also of a son of Abū Sa'd,[6]

[1] Cf. *Misk.*, 378. The ancestors of our Banū Sahl may have been among those whose fortunes were confiscated.

[2] *Yāqūt*, i, 850, 20 f.

[3] L. Massignon (*L'influence de l'Islam*, p. 8) supposes that the Fāṭimid Caliphs had attracted Jewish bankers to Cairo in order to weaken the Caliphate of Baghdād.

[4] See J. Mann, *The Jews in Egypt*, i, 206; *Ibn Duqmāq*, i, 108; *Benjamin of Tudela*, ed. M. N. Adler, London, 1907, p. 98.

[5] *Maqrīzi*, i, 424.

[6] *Ibn Muyassar*, 15, 32; *aṣ-Ṣairafi*, 61; *as-Suyūṭi*, ii, 154.

who, however, does not seem to have taken part in the activities of the firm.

The firm of Sahl Brothers was a family establishment by its organization, a phenomenon by no means rare in Islamic as in European economic history.

Time

We are unable to trace the exact date of their settlement in Fusṭāṭ, and hear of them only after they were already well known. Abū Sa'd and Abū Naṣr came into prominence in the reign of the Caliph al-Ḥākim (996–1021). Even if this is not altogether too early a date, only the last years of al-Ḥākim's reign can come into consideration; for the intolerant policy of this Caliph down to the year 1020 makes it improbable that Jews could have thriven in his capital so freely as to become "famous". Only the restoration, about the year 1020, of religious freedom, and liberty to the forcibly converted to return to Judaism, permitted Jews to emerge once again upon the stage of history. Under al-Ḥākim's successor, aẓ-Ẓāhir, we begin to learn something specific about the activities of the brothers at Fusṭāṭ. During his reign (1021–1036) they must have worked themselves up very rapidly, for we find Abū Sa'd at that time "in the Caliph aẓ-Ẓahir's service" as purveyor.

The Banū Sahl, it appears, continued in the service of aẓ-Ẓāhir throughout the latter's reign, and maintained their economic activities even under the Caliph al-Mustanṣir, when the latter ascended the throne in 1036. Following the death of the Vizier al-Jarjarā'i in 1044 there began the *political* rise of Abū Sa'd, which raised him to the pinnacle of power till he fell a victim to Court intrigues in the year 1047.

Accordingly it can be said with a fair amount of certainty that their period of activity lasted from about 1020 to 1047; and though the concrete data which the sources furnish on the doings of Abū Sa'd and his firm during this period of some twenty-seven years are indeed very meagre, they enable us to determine what constituted the special nature of their economic and political activities.

2. Their Economic Activities

As the starting-point for our inquiry into their economic activities we take the following passage from *Maqrīzi*, i, 424 :—

"In the reign of al-Ḥākim bi-amri-llah there arose two Jewish brothers, of whom one was engaged in commerce, the other in money-changing and the sale of articles which the merchants imported from 'Irāq. These were Abū Sa'd Ibrāhīm and Abū Naṣr Hārūn, the sons of Sahl at-Tustari. They became famous through the part they played in sale transactions and the reporting to heirs of the secret deposits received by them from merchants from near and far, upon the latters' death. This honesty on their part secured them a good name in every land, and accordingly they prospered. And Abū Sa'd Ibrāhīm b. Sahl at-Tustari was in the service of aẓ-Ẓāhir, and purchased for him various kinds of valuables that he required. And he sold him a black female slave, whom aẓ-Ẓāhir took as his favourite, and she gave birth to his son al-Mustanṣir."

From the statement of Maqrīzi we may divide the economic enterprises of the house of Banū Sahl into the following two main spheres of activity :—

1. Dealings in Money.
2. Dealings in Jewels.

Dealings in Money

In accordance with the division of functions practised in the firm of Banū Sahl, only one of the brothers, namely Abū Naṣr Hārūn b. Sahl, devoted himself, as is explicitly stated by Maqrīzi, to money transactions.[1] In his capacity of money-changer and banker Abū Naṣr probably had to perform the manifold functions that fell within the scope of a mediaeval

[1] *Maqrīzi*, i, 424.

banker in Muslim lands. They no doubt covered, as we know was the case elsewhere,[1] not only money-changing transactions but deposits, letters of credit, loans, calculations, and other financial operations.[2] Such transactions probably included, in particular, payment for goods delivered by merchants of 'Irāq and other countries to the firm of Banū Sahl. Differences of exchange in the various countries and the fluctuating values of dirham and dīnār necessitated an exact knowledge of the money market in the interest of correct computation. Moreover, it should not be supposed that payment was always made in cash; it doubtless frequently took the form of cheques or orders on other accounts. It was no doubt part of Abū Naṣr's duties to procure, at the shortest possible notice, the means for financing the commercial undertakings and journeyings of his brother Abū Sa'd, who, as the sources tell us, engaged in commerce (فى التجارة).

It will perhaps seem strange that the sources do not further specify the financial transactions of Abū Naṣr. For example, we hear nothing at all about loans to the Caliph and his Court. But in eleventh-century Egypt we find ourselves at a period of expansion and prosperity, not at one of political and economic decline. Therefore, unlike the firm of Joseph, Aaron and Co., of tenth-century Baghdād, the advancing of loans was probably not the principal branch of this concern. The economic complexion of the Fāṭimid empire was different from that of its 'Abbāsid predecessor. The dealings in cash which had been such a prominent feature of Baghdād society gave place at Cairo to a traffic in valuables, precious stones, and articles of luxury.

[1] Cf. the chapter above on the banking firm of Joseph b. Phineas and Aaron b. Amram.

[2] In Cairo there were in 973 a considerable number of Jewish money-changers, who were organized in a sort of guild. Cf. Maqrīzi, *Itti'āẓ al-Ḥunafā'*, p. 87. Many of the leading members of the Babylonian Jewish community of Fusṭāṭ were, as the Geniza records show, bankers. Cf. *REJ*. 1926, 319.

Dealings in Jewels

C. H. Becker suggests that in eleventh-century Egypt trade in goods held out greater chances of profit than money-lending and the like.[1] It is therefore only natural that purely financial business recedes into the background and trade advances into the forefront of the activities of the establishment of Banū Sahl. The primary requirements of the upper classes at that time were jewels and other valuables. The fascination which beautiful gems had for the Fāṭimid rulers can hardly be described.[2] In effect the sources leave no doubt as to jewels having been one of the main articles in Abū Sa'd's dealings.

The Persian traveller Nāṣir-i-Khosrau[3] simply calls him a "Jewish jeweller" (مردی یهودی بود . . . جوهری); so clearly did he think the trade in jewels the centre of gravity of Abū Sa'd's business.[4]

Through this trade in jewels Abū Sa'd came into contact with the Caliph's Court, and secured himself the position of purveyor to the Court, or Court-Jeweller. For that we have the statement of Nāṣir-i-Khosrau. "There was a Jewish jeweller in Cairo," says he, speaking of Abū Sa'd, "who was a frequent visitor to the sovereign. He was exceedingly rich, and the Caliph placed the greatest trust in him in the purchase of rare gems for himself."[5]

While the sovereign referred to by Nāṣir-i-Khosrau can only have been al-Mustanṣir, in whose reign his journey to Egypt took place, we know from Maqrīzi that Abū Sa'd had already acted in the same capacity for the Caliph aẓ-Ẓāhir :

[1] *Islamstudien*, 1924, i, pp. 213 ff.

[2] One need read only Maqrīzi, i, pp. 408–433, in order to gain, from the list of jewels alone, an idea of the incredible amount of jewels, precious articles, etc., that had accumulated in the treasuries of the Caliph al-Mustanṣir and his predecessors.

[3] *Sefer Nāmeh*, p. 55 ; cf. *Maqrīzi*, i, 337.

[4] Maqrīzi only speaks of Abū Sa'd in general terms as one who engaged in commerce (i, 424) or as a "Jewish Merchant" (i, 355).

[5] *Sefer Nāmeh*, loc. cit.

"Abu Sa'd was in the service of the Caliph aẓ-Ẓāhir and purchased for him the various kinds of valuables he required." [1]

The craving of this monarch for jewels is further described in Maqrīzi's statement that "aẓ-Ẓāhir used to correspond with kings and had purchased a large number of gems".[2] In all probability it was Abū Sa'd and his house, his agents, and his representatives who were charged with this mission.[3]

International Connections

The supplying of objects of value and jewels to the Court lent the firm of Abū Sa'd the character of an international enterprise. If C. H. Becker [4] details as the principal spheres of Egypt's foreign trade in the Middle Ages (*a*) trade with Nūbia and the Sūdān, (*b*) the Indian transit trade, and (*c*) the trade of the Mediterranean, these were also, no doubt, the fields in which our Jewish firm and its agents conducted their activities abroad. In supplying the Caliph and his Court they had to make use of connections with other countries of the Orient,[5] undertaking long journeys and bringing the desired articles from distant places. Not only does this follow

[1] *Maqrīzi*, i, 424.

[2] Op. cit., i, 355.

[3] Almost all the sources contain tallying reports of Abū Sa'd's having supplied a slave-girl to the Caliph aẓ-Ẓāhir. The reason why this circumstance is specially stressed is because this black slave became the mother of aẓ-Ẓāhir's successor al-Mustanṣir. *Maqrīzi*, i, 355; i, 424–5, says: "The mother of the Caliph al-Mustanṣir was a black slave that had belonged to a Jewish merchant named Abū Sa'd Sahl b. Aaron at-Tustari; she was bought from him by aẓ-Ẓāhir, and al-Mustanṣir was born of her." It is of importance to note that this slave-girl was bought from Abū Sa'd by the Caliph. However, as only one deal of this sort is recorded in our historical documents, it may safely be inferred that this was a special favour done to the Caliph, and not an ordinary transaction in one of the firm's usual articles of trade. The black slave-girl had obviously been the concubine of Abū Sa'd. On the question of slave-trade by Jews in European Middle Ages cf. I. Abrahams, *Jewish Life in the Middle Ages*, 2nd ed., London, 1932, pp. 111 ff.

[4] *Islamstudien*, 1922, i, p. 185.

[5] No details are available as to the manner in which these business trips were arranged.

from the nature of their commissions but Maqrīzi states explicitly that our firm had dealings with "merchants from near and far" من التجار فى القرب والبعد, and that, thanks to their scrupulous business ethics and integrity, they enjoyed a good reputation "everywhere", or "in every land" (فى الافاق).[1] Letters addressed to them, of which fragments are preserved in the Geniza,[2] from Palestine, 'Irāq, Rūm, etc., testify to the reputation they enjoyed far beyond the borders of Egypt, and even of the Fāṭimid dominions. Although this correspondence deals with purely Jewish matters (assistance to the poor, ransom of captives, erection of a synagogue, etc.), it may be supposed that the communities concerned were also commercially connected with the recipients. A Geniza document mentions Jews in Cairo who had relatives in South Arabia and India, and the editor remarks [3] that "there seems to have been a group of Cairene Jews settled at Aden . . . and engaged in the trade with India and Ceylon". Though our Arabic sources make no reference to these, it may be asked whether they may not have been agents or representatives of the firm of Banū Sahl.

Maqrīzi makes special mention of the Banū Sahl's relations "with the merchants of 'Irāq". The Babylonian-'Irāqi community of Cairo constituted a natural base for the cultivation of economic relations between 'Irāq and Egypt, and performed a very pertinent economic function in the exchange of goods and wares between the two countries. The leading rôle which Abū Sa'd and his brother, as we know, played within this group was essentially economic. They were the obvious intermediaries of all the trade that came to Cairo from or via 'Irāq. No doubt they were also the agents of the large Baghdād firms which, as we learn from Maqrīzi,[4] placed large deposits of goods, and perhaps of money too, with them.

[1] *Maqrīzi*, i, 424.
[2] Cf. J. Mann, *Texts and Studies*, i, 118, 180; *The Jews in Egypt*, i, 87–94.
[3] *Geniza-Fragments*, ed. Gottheil-Worrel, pp. xxiv, 45–57, 142–8.
[4] *Maqrīzi*, i, 424.

Wealth

The sources afford us an idea not only of the international character of the firm of Abū Sa'd, but also of their extraordinary wealth, obviously due to profits from dealings in money, gems, etc. What their margin of profit or percentage of loss may have been we do not know, but the final result was such riches that the sources seem unable to praise them too highly.

Nāṣir-i-Khosrau, during his sojourn in Cairo in the years 1047–8, heard so much about Abū Sa'd's wealth that he writes: "He is exceedingly rich. God alone knows how great his fortune is," and adds the following illustration: "It is said that 300 silver vases stood on the verandah of his house, each with a tree planted in it. The great number of these trees, all of them laden with fruit, lent to his verandah the appearance of a garden." [1]

Another report on the riches of the Banū Sahl is cited from كتاب الذخائر [2] by Maqrīzi. In two different passages there is a description of a gift [3] presented by Abū Sa'd to the Caliph's mother in the year 1044 (436) on the occasion of his being appointed to a new office. The gift in question was a silver ship which actually became a legend and was simply called عشارى.[4] The Arabic sources are enthusiastic in its praise. Abū Sa'd is said to have spent 2,400 dīnārs on it alone, whilst tapestries, gilding, and the work in silver cost over 130,000 silver dirhams. The memory of the donor had

[1] *Nāṣir-i-Khosrau*, pp. 55–6. For a similar description cf. *Maqrīzi*, i, 479, and i, 424.

[2] The author of this work was mainly interested in the treasures and valuables of the Fāṭimids, and is frequently cited by Qalqashandi and Maqrīzi. Cf. C. H. Becker, *Beiträge*, i, 21.

[3] *Maqrīzi*, i, 475, 51; cf. ibid., p. 416; the divergences in details between the texts are irrelevant for our purpose. Cf. further F. Wuestenfeld, *Gesch. d. Fatimidenchalifen*, 230; Lane-Poole, p. 148.

[4] This word occurs frequently in Maqrīzi; de Sacy, *Chresth. Arabe*, ii, 114, note 52, explains it as " une espèce de barque employée sur le Nil ". Cf. Dozy, *Supplément*.

not yet been forgotten when in 1068, long after his death, this treasure was looted by the greedy Turkish troops together with the rest of the contents of the storehouse of the Caliph al-Mustanṣir.[1]

A man who could afford to make such a gift must have had vast means at his disposal.

A third testimony shows that the economic capacity of the firm was still practically unlimited in the year 1047. Following the murder of his brother Abū Sa'd, Abū Naṣr, according to Nāṣir-i-Khosrau,[2] offered al-Mustanṣir nothing less for his own security than a gift of 200,000 Maghribi dīnārs cash for the Caliph's privy purse.[3] The Caliph, it is true, did not accept the offer, but its magnitude is symptomatic of the firm's position.[4]

3. The Political Rise of Abū Sa'd

Abū Sa'd's relations with the Court, so far as we have seen, had hitherto been purely economic and commercial; his duty was to satisfy the Caliph's demands for rarities and the like. But a decisive change took place in these relations upon the death of aẓ-Ẓāhir. For on aẓ-Ẓāhir's demise in the year 1036 the regency of the realm was taken over, on behalf of his seven-year-old successor al-Mustanṣir, by the latter's

[1] When the Turks in 1068 wished to sell the plundered articles by auction the jewellers of Cairo were not even able to estimate their respective values.

[2] Op. cit., 55–6.

[3] The solvency of the firm of the Sahl Brothers is astonishing. According to *Ibn Muyassar*, 3, 13, Abū Naṣr's entire fortune was subsequently confiscated. It would be of importance for the economic historian to gain some notion of the magnitude of fortunes in the Islamic Middle Ages. For conditions in Europe at the time cf. Strieder, *Zur Genesis des modernen Kapitalismus*, 1904 (*contra* Sombart); F. Schipper, *Anfaenge des Kapitalismus bei den abendlaendischen Juden*, 1907; R. Haepke, "Die Entstehung der grossen buergerlichen Vermoegen im Mittelalter" (*Schmollers Jahrbuch*, Bd. 29, pp. 235–271).

[4] That both these Jews also assisted their co-religionists, contributing generously to the support of the poor, appears from the Geniza texts. Cf. Mann, *Texts*, 373.

mother,[1] the very woman who had once been sold to aẓ-Ẓāhir as a black slave-girl. One of her first acts, the sources tell us, was to summon her former master Abū Sa'd, to whom she owed her present position, to Court, and appoint him to a high *political* office. This happened about 428/1036. Abū Sa'd's connection with the Court, till now primarily derived from the sphere of economics, thereby began to extend to politics as well. He was destined to become ever more involved in politics, leading to a singular political career. And following the death in 436/1044 of the Vizier al-Jarjarā'i, his political powers increased greatly.

To what position was Abū Sa'd appointed, and what was the political office with which he was invested at the Court of the Dowager Regent? The sources speak in general terms of "a high rank" (درجة عليّة) to which Abū Sa'd was promoted by her upon the death of aẓ-Ẓāhir.[2] According to Ibn Muyassar,[3] "the influence of Abū Sa'd extended in the government"; according to Ibn aṣ-Ṣairafi [4] he became "inspector of all the affairs of the State"; and as-Suyūṭi [5] goes so far as to say that he controlled the State.

All these general expressions, however, tell us nothing about the concrete function of Abū Sa'd within the Fāṭimid administration. It is indeed not easy to determine the exact nature of his position, owing to the very great divergencies between the texts regarding the designation and terminology of Abū Sa'd's office and title.

(*a*) Ibn aṭ-Ṭuwair,[6] quoted by Qalqashandi, calls him

[1] Thus we read in *Ibn al-Athīr*, x, 55; in *Ibn Taghribirdi*, ii, 183. Cf. also *Maqrīzi*, i, 355. Her name does not appear anywhere in the sources. Before her coming to Court she figures as جارية سوداء, a black slave-girl; later as والدة المستنصر or امّ المستنصر "the mother of al-Mustanṣir".

[2] *Ibn Muyassar*, p. 1, 7. See also *Maqrīzi*, i, 424.

[3] Loc. cit., 1, 9.

[4] *Ibn aṣ-Ṣairafi*, 75, 3: وعظم شأنه الى ان صار ناظرا فى جميع امور الدولة.

[5] *Ḥusn al-Muḥāḍara*, ii, 153.

[6] Ibn aṭ-Ṭuwair is, along with Musabbiḥi, an authority frequently cited by both Qalqashandi and Maqrīzi. His book on the Fāṭimid dynasty is not extant. With regard to him see Becker, *Beiträge*, 29; Bjoerkmann, *Beiträge*, 83.

"vizier" and includes him in the list of the viziers of the Fāṭimid rulers who attained to fame.[1] This statement, however, is not borne out by the facts. Abū Sa'd, it is true, influenced the affairs of state to a far greater extent than, say, the vizier al-Fallāḥi, who was in office at that time.[1]

Nevertheless, it is certain that Abū Sa'd was never appointed to the office of vizier in the sense meant by Ibn aṭ-Ṭuwair. He was not nominated for this rank like the others whom Ibn aṭ-Ṭuwair mentions together with him. The sources unequivocally distinguish Abū Sa'd from the official vizier,[2] and significantly enough he is not mentioned in the very full lists of viziers of the Fāṭimid house given by Ibn Muyassar,[3] Maqrīzi,[4] or as-Suyūṭi.[5]

(*b*) But according to Maqrīzi, Abū Sa'd was appointed to a different office, that of وساطة.[6] The nature of this office has not yet been clearly elucidated. It appears to have been a purely Fāṭimid institution probably dating from the time of the Caliph al-Ḥākim.[7] The term is not infrequently used by the Egyptian historians.[8] From Ibn aṣ-Ṣairafi it would appear that the incumbent of the office of *wisāṭa* was charged with duties connected with army administration.[9]

Qalqashandi[10] informs us, concerning the line of

[1] *Ṣubḥ al-A'shā*, iii, p. 489.

[2] *Ibn aṣ-Ṣairafi*, 75, 4; *Maqrīzi*, i, 424. The sources show that Abū Sa'd was always conflicting with the official vizier, over whom he exercised control.

[3] Loc. cit., p. 31, 23.

[4] Loc. cit., ii, 92, 117.

[5] *Ḥusn al-Muḥāḍara*, ii, 147 ff. Cf. Zambaur, *Manuel*, p. 96; Wuestenfeld, *Geschichte der Fatimidenchalifen*, p. 252.

[6] *Maqr.*, i, 497, 11.

[7] Ibn 'Ammār seems to have been the first bearer of this title at the time of al-Ḥākim.

[8] Cf. *Ibn aṣ-Ṣairafi*, 78, 12; 79, 2, 7, 9, 13; 80, 7, 10; etc. Cf. also *Ibn al-Athīr*, ix, 83.

[9] de Sacy, *Chrest. Arabe*, ii, 91, has collected valuable material for the history of this conception. Cf. also Fagnan, *Additions aux dictionnaires arabes*, Algiers, 1923, 186; cf. Freytag, *Lexicon*, iv, 464.

[10] Op. cit., iii, 489. Bjoerkman, *Beiträge*, p. 111, explains *wāsita* as "eine Art Wesier". al-Māwardi gives further details of this title; cf. Constit. Polit., pp. 41, 148, 425.

demarcation between " vizier " and " wāsiṭa ", that وساطة فى رتبة دون الوزارة.

(c) Analysis of the sources leads us to yet another designation of Abū Sa'd's function. In Ibn Muyassar [1] we read: " The mother of the Caliph made her (former) master Abū Sa'd vizier." This would confirm Qalqashandi's version that Abū Sa'd became vizier, but we hear that the mother of the Caliph appointed Abū Sa'd to be " her vizier " when appointing the vizier al-Fallāḥi as vizier for her son, the Caliph.[2] This passage leaves no doubt that there were at this time two viziers, a " vizier for the Caliph " and a " vizier for the Caliph's mother ". The terminological distinction has the support of Ibn al-Athīr,[3] who says of Abū Sa'd وصار وزيرا لها " he became vizier to her ", i.e. to the Caliph's mother in contrast to the Caliph himself.

Here we are in the presence of quite a new administrative creation, as a duality in the office of vizier in such a form is not rooted in the theory of political administration. And this was the office bestowed upon the Jew Abū Sa'd, the Dowager's favourite. To serve her own purposes she must have built up an administrative machinery, for the direction of which a special official was needed.[4] In effect we do hear of a " Dīwān of the Caliph's mother " [5] and of " affairs of the Caliph's mother ",[6] as well as of special tasks and duties with whose execution and discharge " her vizier " was entrusted. " Abū Sa'd had charge of the affairs that specifically concerned the Caliph's mother," says Ibn aṣ-Ṣairafi [7]; and similarly

[1] Loc. cit., p. 14.

[2] *Ibn Taghribirdi*, ii, 184, 3.

[3] *Ibn al-Athīr*, x, 55.

[4] This office of a private vizier for the mother also continued to exist after Abū Sa'd's death, when al-Yāzūri became " Vizier of the Caliph's mother ". Cf. *Ibn Muyassar*, p. 8; cf. p. 32.

[5] *Ibn Muyassar*, pp. 1, 10; 5, 13.

[6] *Ibn Muyassar*, pp. 8–9.

[7] *Ibn aṣ-Ṣairafi*, p. 75, 3.

Ibn Muyassar,[1] " he was connected with the service of the Caliph's mother " ; while Maqrīzi [2] also makes it plain that Abū Sa'd was employed by that lady in her particular affairs.

Special Political Mission

But what were these particular affairs and functions which constituted the special political mission of Abū Sa'd on behalf of the Caliph's mother ? The accounts of the Arab historians make it evident that the internal politics of the Courts of the Fāṭimid rulers at that period was rife with friction between two military bodies at Cairo : the Turkish mercenaries, on the one hand, and regiments of black slaves on the other. Although there had already been negro regiments at Cairo in earlier times, they had never formed such a separate organization, in opposition to other military units, as they did in the eleventh century. The history of the black regiments does not concern us here : what is relevant is that at the time of al-Mustanṣir there existed between them and the Turkish mercenaries an open conflict which shook the structure of the state to its foundations and ultimately brought it to the brink of destruction.[3] Ibn Taghribirdi ascribes the decline of the Fāṭimid empire to this very cause.[4]

This conflict between Negro and Turkish regiments, this dualism in the military administration, deserves special attention because it reacted upon the structure of the civil administration. For each section of the army had its patrons among the highest dignitaries of the civil administration. The Caliph and the " Vizier of the Caliph " seem to have supported

[1] Op. cit., p. 8.

[2] i, 424.

[3] O'Leary, *A Short History of the Fatimid Caliphate*, p. 196 : " For six years following (1044/1055) the domestic politics of Egypt centred entirely in the struggle between the Turkish mercenaries and the negro troops." Lane-Poole, op. cit., p. 145 : " Meanwhile the jealousy between the Turkish troops and the Sudani battalions . . . grew to alarming proportions."

[4] ii, 182, 17.

and protected the Turks, whilst the Caliph's mother and the "Vizier of the Caliph's mother" favoured the negro battalions.

The Arabic sources make it plain that the Queen Mother made the black troops "her special concern". Having herself originally been brought to Court as a black slave, she did everything upon coming to power to reinforce and augment the existing regiments of men of her own race.[1] The sources state that the Caliph's mother was the cause of the augmentation of the black regiments, and that "her fondness for this race was well known".[2]

Her object was obviously to strengthen her power at home by employing the black troops as her own bodyguard and as an instrument of her policy and power.[3]

This explains the specific function of Abū Sa'd. As "the Vizier of the Queen Mother", he had to aid her in the attainment of her political and military ends. For she required co-workers and assistants in the prosecution of her slave policy. And who could have been more suitable for this office than Abū Sa'd, the Purveyor to the Court, who had the necessary capital at his disposal, with all the requisite experience and connections, and who was, in addition, the Queen Mother's former master, to whom she owed all her power and in whom she consequently had every confidence? Upon his appointment as "her" vizier, and in the political advancement that followed, his principal duties were connected with the execution of the political and military policy of his mistress.

It is obvious that the growth in the power of the blacks could only be viewed with apprehension by the Turks. The conflict between both military bodies was therefore inevitable. The

[1] *Ibn Muyassar*, 13, 18; 14, 4.

[2] *Maqrīzi*, i, 355; also *Ibn Taghribirdi*, ii, 183, 19, speaks of ميل امّ المستنصر اليهم. *Maqr.*, i, 335: وعرفت رغبتها في هذا الجنس.

[3] The Caliph's mother had a bodyguard of her own, numbering more than 50,000 (*Ibn Muyassar*, 35, 8). She also attended to the purchase of the black slaves (*Ibn Muyassar*, 13–14), and according to Maqrīzi, i, 355, "she had them bought everywhere."

negro policy of the Queen Mother therefore involved Abū Sa'd in the most dangerous intrigues at Court, and moved him into the forefront of Court affairs. And for this we have, indeed, direct and unambiguous testimony. Maqrīzi says: "The mother of al-Mustanṣir, who ruled over the realm, being ill-disposed towards the Turks, incited her (former) master Abū Sa'd at-Tustari to exterminate them; and the negroes were strengthened in consequence." [1]

This proves the relationship between Abū Sa'd and the military policy of Fāṭimid Egypt in the reign of al-Mustanṣir, and explains the nature of his political activities as "Vizier to the Queen Mother", which raised him to the highest pinnacle of power in the state.

The Murder of Abū Sa'd

At the height of his power, however, Abū Sa'd had to pay with death for his prominence and for the perilous duties he performed on behalf of the Caliph's mother. The Turkish troops—it is highly significant that they were the ones concerned—against whom his mission and the entire policy of the Queen Mother were directed, attacked and murdered him in the year 439/1047.

It must have been a sensational event when the soldiers of al-Mustanṣir, as Nāṣir-i-Khosrau reports, having committed the murder,[2] mounted their horses and gathered, 20,000 strong, on the Maidān of Cairo.[3] Fearing the punishment of the Caliph they waited on horseback until midday. "We are the servants of the Caliph, but we have committed a murder," was the message they sent to al-Mustanṣir, who finally ordered them to withdraw.[4]

[1] *Maqrīzi*, i, 335: وحثّت على قتلهم مولاها ابا سعد التسترى فقويت العبيد لذلك

[2] Op. cit., pp. 55–6, does not give the precise date; he speaks only of "one day"; *Ibn Muyassar*, 2, 4, mentions the murder, under 439/1047, as occurring in the month of Jumādā I.

[3] Regarding the scene of the deed, cf. also *Ibn aṣ-Ṣairafi*, 75, 6; *Ibn Muyassar*, 2, 3; *Maqrīzi*, i, 424.

[4] Details of the terrible manner in which Abū Sa'd was executed and buried are given by *Ibn aṣ-Ṣairafi*, 75, 6, and *Ibn Muyassar*, 2, 5.

The sources enable us to look behind the scenes and show that the murder was planned and prepared with system and thoroughness. The instigator was Abū Sa'd's rival al-Fallāḥi, who incited the Turkish troops against him until they murdered him.[1] The motives by which al-Fallāḥi was actuated were both political and personal. The political motives are obvious from what has been related above regarding the dualism of the military administration. The personal ones arose from the dualism in the civil administration, the double vizierate. This official vizier of the Caliph, al-Fallāḥi, felt cramped by the Jewish favourite Abū Sa'd, through whom his competence was so restricted that, as we are told, he was completely subordinate to the other, possessing "neither command nor veto, but only the name of vizier".[2]

What the death of Abū Sa'd meant to the Caliph's mother is evident from the vengeance she exacted of al-Fallāḥi. She was filled with hatred against the perpetrator of the murder of "her vizier", and would not rest until the Caliph dismissed him and had him put to death[3] in 440/1048.

Nevertheless, the Dowager persevered in the pursuit of her politico-military designs. Far from giving up her separate administrative machinery upon the death of the Jew Abū Sa'd of Tustar,[4] she appointed the judge Abū Muḥammad Ḥasan al-Yāzūri[5] "to be her vizier"[6] on the advice of her court officials. He was entrusted with all the duties and functions[7] previously discharged by Abū Sa'd at-Tustari.[8]

[1] *Ibn Muyassar*, 1, 10; 14, 3. *Ibn aṣ-Ṣairafi*, 75, 5. *Ibn al-Athīr*, x, 55. *Ibn Taghrib.*, ii, 184.

[2] *Ibn Muyassar*, 1, 9; *Ibn aṣ-Ṣairafi*, 75, 4.

[3] *Ibn Muyassar*, 2, 9. Cf. *Ibn Muyassar*, 4, 6; *Ibn aṣ-Ṣairafi*, 75, 8; *Maqrīzi*, i, 335; *Ibn Taghribirdi*, ii, 184.

[4] Cf. *Ibn Muyassar*, 8, 21, and *Ibn aṣ-Ṣairafi*, 73, 7.

[5] *Ibn aṣ-Ṣairafi*, 73; *Ibn Muyassar*, 2, 17.

[6] *Ibn Muyassar*, 9, 1: ان يكون وزيرها.

[7] *Ibn aṣ-Ṣairafi*, 73, 5; *Ibn Muyassar*, 5, 13; cf. *Ibn Muyassar*, 2, 17. We find the same administrative terminology used regarding al-Yāzūri as for Abū Sa'd.

[8] For note see p. 86.

We have hitherto left Abū Naṣr, the brother of Abū Sa'd, unmentioned for the reason that he had, as far as the sources show, no share in Abū Sa'd's *political* rise. Upon the latter's entry into politics Abū Naṣr probably had to shoulder the entire responsibility for the economic affairs of the firm by himself. That he had also had some connection with Court affairs in previous times is, nevertheless, probable, and for this the insulting incident related by *Maqrīzi*, i, 424, would seem to provide some confirmation.[1]

But after the murder of his brother he is again mentioned. According to Nāṣir-i-Khosrau, Abū Naṣr, hearing of the tragic fate of his brother, hastened to write to the Caliph offering him a gift of 200,000 dīnārs in exchange for a charter; but not only did the Caliph not accept the sum, he publicly tore up the letter and informed Abū Naṣr: "Be not afraid and return to thy house. Nobody has any claims against thee; while as regards the money I do not require it." Nāṣir-i-Khosrau adds that the Caliph granted both him and his nephew, the son of Abū Sa'd, a safe conduct.[2]

J. Mann[3] concluded from the Geniza fragments that it is evident that both brothers were killed on the same day and that "he (Naṣr) must also have fallen victim on the day when the Turkish bodyguard assassinated his brother Abū Sa'd". This is, however, by no means supported by the

[8] As long as the Caliph's mother maintained an independent administration, the differences between the Turkish and the negro troops also remained. This finally led to a pitched battle between them at Kūm Sharīk.

[1] In *Maqrīzi*, i, 424, we read: "Abū Naṣr, the brother of Abū Sa'd, betook him to the vizier Ibn al-Anbāri, but was insolently received by one of the latter's attendants. Abū Naṣr thought that if he reported this behaviour to Ibn al-Anbāri the vizier would express indignation at it and apologize for it. It happened otherwise than he expected, however, and Abū Naṣr complained to his brother Abū Sa'd. . . . The latter interceded with the Caliph's mother and with the Caliph, and Ibn al-Anbāri was shortly after dismissed." This probably took place in the year 1044.

[2] *Sefer Nāmeh*, 55–6.

[3] J. Mann, *The Jews in Palestine and Egypt*, i, 78, 82.

Arabic sources. On the contrary, in addition to the statement of Nāṣir-i-Khosrau to which we have just referred, there is also the testimony of Ibn Muyassar, according to which Abū Naṣr remained connected with the Caliph after his brother's death and even performed certain political duties in connection with the struggles in Aleppo and Damascus.[1] The Arabic sources only go to show that his own time was not far distant. We hear that his entire fortune was confiscated and that he was tortured until he died.[2] His death seems to have occurred in the year 440/1048, some months after that of his brother.

The son of Abū Sa'd, Abū 'Ali Ḥasan b. Abī Sa'd Ibrāhīm b. Sahl at-Tustari, on the other hand, does not seem to have been hindered in the official career upon which he had embarked. He was employed "in one of the Dīwāns" and even appointed vizier [3] by al-Mustanṣir towards the end of the year 456/1064, probably after his conversion to Islam. This office, however, he occupied for a very short period only.[4]

[1] *Ibn Muyassar*, 2, 9, and 3.

[2] Loc. cit., 3.

[3] According to *Ibn aṣ-Ṣairafi*, p. 61, 5, he was put in charge of the بيت المال. *Ibn Muyassar*, 15; 32, 20; *as-Suyūṭi*, ii, 154. *Ibn Muyassar*, 32, 20, says of him كان يهوديا واسلم; cf. *Ibn aṣ-Ṣairafi*, 61, 5. Hence J. Mann's question, loc. cit., i, 78, as to whether the son of Abū Sa'd remained a Jew, is answered in the negative by the Arabic sources.

[4] The end of Abū Sa'd and his brother Abū Naṣr does not seem to have had consequences for Egyptian Jewry. We hear nothing of any provisions limiting or weakening Jewish influence in the Fāṭimid administration. As before, Jews possessed of the necessary qualifications could attain high positions in Government service. At the beginning of the twelfth century we again meet a Jew, named Abu'l-Munajjā b. Sha'yā al-yahūdi, ابو المنجا بن شيعا اليهودى, serving under the Vizier al-Afḍal Shāhānshāh (1089/1121) in the responsible post of مشارف الاعمال الشرقية, i.e. Inspector of the Damietta District. It is reported (in *Maqrīzi*, i, 72, 477, 487–8, and in *Ibn Duqmāq*, ed. Vollers, ii, pp. 46–7; also cf. Ibn Iyās, *Ta'rīkh*, i, 46; *Khalīl aẓ-Ẓāhiri*, p. 34, 9) that he had a Nile canal constructed which considerably advanced the development of agriculture. The planters approached him as head of the Department of Agriculture with a petition for the irrigation of a certain area, and

It cannot be affirmed with certainty that the fact of Abū Sa'd's being a Jew was used as a cause for incitement against him. But, in any case, it was the memory of the *Jew* Abū Sa'd which was preserved for posterity. A poet by the name of Riḍa b. Thaub,[1] probably of Damascus, made himself the mouthpiece of the current feeling in Cairo. Some of his satirical verses have been handed down to us, and they are probably an approximate echo of a period at which the Jew Abū Sa'd was living and active in Cairo. The verses [2] are as follows :—

al-Afḍal granted permission to dig a canal for the purpose. Work on the canal, under the supervision and direction of Abu'l-Munajjā, took six years, and it was opened by al-Afḍal in the year 506/1112. The canal was named خليج ابى المنجا after its constructor. But Abu'l-Munajjā fell into disfavour on account of the high costs of construction, and was sent to prison in Alexandria. The name of the canal he had built was changed and it was called after al-Afḍal البحر الافضلى. It is not uninteresting to learn that this change of name proved unsuccessful, as the public continued to call it the Abu'l-Munajjā canal. The sources inform us that Abu'l-Munajjā suffered considerably in prison, and hoped to bring his life to an end by the following action. He wrote a copy of the Qur'ān, ending it with the words : "Written by Abu'l-Munajjā the Jew." When this copy reached the Alexandria market it aroused considerable attention. An inquiry was held at which Abu'l-Munajjā explained the reason for his action and was thereupon set at liberty. What happened to him afterwards is not stated. Among the Geniza fragments are Hebrew poems in his honour ; and he is ascribed the title " the exalted one of the State " (סני אלדולה), as well as "prince of the princes of Yeshurun " (שר שרי ישורון). Cf. Mann, *Jews in Egypt*, i, pp. 215–17 ; ii, pp. 264–9, 382. From *Ibn Muyassar*, p. 74, 4, we learn of yet another important Jewish official, named Ibn Abi'd-Dimm (ابن ابى الدمّ اليهودى) in the service of the Fāṭimids. It appears that in 524/1130 he was the secretary of the ديوان الانشاء at the time of the Caliph al-'Āmir. We are also informed, in *Ibn Muyassar*, 42, 7, of a certain Ibn Kūjik (ابن كوجك اليهودى) who served in the ديوان التحقيق in 624/1227.

[1] Such is the reading of H. Massé in *Ibn Muyassar*, p. xxi ; Blochet (*Histoire d'Egypte*, p. 22) reads Rāḍi b. Nāīb, and G. Wiet (*Journ. Asiat.* 1921, vol. 18, p. 95) suggests Ibn Ayyūb.

[2] These lines occur in *Ibn Muyassar*, p. 2 ; also in as-Suyūṭi, *Ḥusn al-Muḥāḍara*, ii, 153 ; and probably frequently elsewhere in Arabic literature. They are applied to various periods and events. European historians often connect them with Ya'qūb b. Killis ; cf. v. Kremer, *Kulturgeschichte*, i,

"The Jews [1] of these times do a rank attain,
The goal of their desires ; for now they reign.
Theirs is the power, wealth to them doth cling,
To them belong both councillor and king.
Egyptians ! Hear the words I counsel you :
Turn Jews, for heaven itself has turned a Jew." [2]

188 ; J. Mann, *The Jews in Egypt*, i, 16–17, etc. Contrast, however, Mez, *Renaissance*, p. 53. In *Ibn Muyassar* they are clearly applied to our period. These verses became a standard article for use whenever anti-Jewish feeling began to rise high. We find them employed again by the Persian historian Waṣṣāf against Sa'd ad-Daula, the next object of our study.

[1] It is probable, judging from the plural, that the poet's ill-feeling extended also to Abū Manṣūr Ṣadaqa al-Fallāḥi, the Vizier responsible for Abū Sa'd's death, who was himself a converted Jew. Doubtless there were other high officials of Jewish origin at the Court. *Ibn aṣ-Ṣairafi*, p. 76, who gives a biography of al-Fallāḥi, tells nothing of him prior to his conversion. Cf. *as-Suyūṭi*, ii, p. 152.

[2] Quoted according to E. G. Browne, *Persian Literature under Tartar Dominion*, iii, p. 31, with slight changes.

C. UNDER THE MONGOL ĪL-KHĀNS

I. SA'D AD-DAULA

IN surveying the sources for information on outstanding Jews in the political and economic life of the Islamic Middle Ages, we meet with one other leading Jewish personality only during the thirteenth century in the empire of the Mongol Īl-Khāns. This is the Jewish Vizier and physician Sa'd ad-Daula, whose influence on political and economic events of his period reached far beyond his own immediate surroundings.

The information hitherto at our disposal concerning Sa'd ad-Daula was derived primarily from the Persian historian Waṣṣāf, who was used by the well-known European scholars in their historical works on the Mongol period.[1] But within the limits of their general accounts those authors could offer no more than a rough and sketchy picture of the activities of Sa'd ad-Daula.

New sources,[2] however, have become available since the

[1] For a general account of the Īl-Khāns see: Hammer-Purgstall, *Geschichte der Ilkhane*, Darmstadt, 1842–3; M. d'Ohsson, *Histoire des Mongols depuis Tschinguiz Khan jusqu'à Timour Bey ou Tamerlan*, Hague and Amsterdam, 1834–5; H. Howorth, *History of the Mongols*, London, 1876–1888; E. G. Browne, *Persian Literature under Tartar Dominion*, Cambridge, 1920.

[2] In *Waṣṣāf* the chapter dealing with Sa'd ad-Daula in the used MS. Add. 23517 is found on fols. 196*a*–207*a*. All quotations from the MS. of *Rashīd ad-Dīn* are to be found in the chapter of MS. Add. 16688 on fols. 148*b*–156*a*. Cf. on the various MSS. of his history, E. G. Browne, "Suggestions for a complete edition of the Jami'ut-tawārikh of Rashīd ad-Dīn," *JRAS.*, 1908, pp. 17–37. The short report on Sa'd ad-Daula in Khwāndamīr, *Ḥabību's-Siyar*, iii, pp. 44–7, is obviously taken from Rashīd ad-Dīn. Considering the large number of historical works on the period of the Īl-Khāns it is very probable that later Persian authors, primarily Ḥāfiẓ Abrū, Mirkhwānd, etc., also deal with Sa'd ad-Daula. In addition to these Persian sources the Syriac Chronicle of Bar Hebræus and various Arabic authorities cited in the text were used.

publication of those histories, and first and foremost the Arabic chronicle of Ibn al-Fuwaṭi, which have considerably enriched our store of information about Sa'd ad-Daula, and make it possible for us to reach a clear and objective estimate of this phenomenon of a Jewish Vizier serving a heathen Mongol emperor.

1. Historical Background

In dealing with Sa'd ad-Daula we turn from the sphere of the Caliphate, to which our inquiry has hitherto been confined, to the Mongol Īl-Khān Arghūn (1284/1291). After the triumphal march of Hūlāgū and the expansion of his rule subsequent to the fall of Baghdād in 1258, Islam lost its dominant position in the Eastern provinces of the Caliphate and became a religion among all the others. In virtue of the principle of tolerance for all faiths, maintained by the Īl-Khāns, the concept of the "Protected People", the *ahl adh-Dhimma* was deprived of its former importance; with it fell the extremely varied professional restrictions into which it had expanded, and primarily those regarding the admission of Jews and Christians to government posts.

Bar Hebræus, the Christian historian of the thirteenth century, expresses the changed values produced by the Mongols in telling fashion thus: "With the Mongols there is neither slave nor free man, neither believer nor pagan, neither Christian nor Jew; but they regard all men as belonging to one and the same stock."[1]

For Christian and Jews, the two groups chiefly affected by the *ahl adh-Dhimma* policy, current until then, this change in constitutional and religious principles implied a considerable

[1] *Chronicon Syriacum*, p. 490, f. 575. In the following pages all quotations from Bar Hebræus are made from the edition of Budge; "p." refers to the translation, "f." to the Syrian text. Cf. also Ghāzi b. al-Wāsiṭi, fol. 27*a*–*b* (p. 449): "A firmān of the Īl-Khān (Hūlāgū) had appeared to the effect that everyone should have the right to profane his faith openly and his religious connection; and that the members of one religious body should not oppose those of another."

amelioration of their position ; whereas for the Muslims it meant that they had sunk to a depth hitherto unknown in their history.

The *Oriental church*, which had expended its energies ever since the Arab Conquest in a prolonged struggle against the opposed religious forces, found itself able to abandon its defensive position under Arghūn.[1] Arghūn's tolerance toward the Christians must have been greatly increased by political considerations. For, following the policy of expansion introduced by his father Abāqā, Arghūn also tried to utilize the influence of Oriental Christianity in order to win the aid of European Christendom for the *one* great political task which he and his father had set themselves, namely, the liberation of Palestine and Syria from the Mamelūk sway. To this end Arghūn sent Nestorian emissaries [2] to the Courts of the Christian kings of Europe and the Pope in order to persuade them to nothing less than a common Christian-Mongolian crusade against Islam.[3] To Arghūn the destruction of the Mamelūk power seemed so important that in an epistle to the Christian powers he even declared himself ready to adopt Christianity when Jerusalem would be retrieved

[1] F. S. Assemani, *Bibliotheca Orientalis Clementino-Vaticane*, Roma, 1719–1728. See L. Browne, *The Eclipse of Christianity in Asia*, Cambridge, 1933 ; F. Labourt, *Le Christianisme dans l'empire perse*, Paris, 1904, p. 350 : " À ce moment l'Église nestorienne atteignit sa plus grande expansion territoriale."

[2] We have detailed reports from the emissaries themselves regarding the delegations to Europe at the time of Arghūn. See the Syriac edition of this report by P. Bedjan, and the translation by J. B. Chabot, *Histoire de Mar Jab'allaha*, iii, Paris, 1895. Cf. also J. A. Montgomery, *The History of Jab'allaha*, iii, New York, 1927 (one part only). E. W. Budge, *The Monks of Kublai Khan*, London, 1928.

[3] Of the relationships between the Mongols and Europe in the thirteenth and fourteenth centuries an excellent account is given in the still classical study of Abel-Rémusat, *Memoire sur les relations politiques des princes chrétiens avec les empereurs Mongols*, in *Mem. de l'Acad. Royale des Inscript. et Belles-Lettres*, Paris, 1821–2, vols. vi and vii ; also in P. Pelliot, " Les Mongols et la Papauté," *Revue de l'Orient Chrétien*, vols. 23, 24, 28, and Chabot, " Notes sur les relations du roi Arghūn avec l'Occident," pp. 187–248 (appendix i to *Histoire de Mar Jab'allaha*, iv, Paris, 1895).

from Islam.[1] Had this daring idea been realized, Christianity might have become the religion of Asia.[2] The fact that this, the greatest opportunity afforded the Christian religion, was never exploited is regarded by historians as the major failure of Christendom.[3]

During this epoch, which was so marked with spiritual tension, *Oriental Jewry* also experienced an unexpected although no more than temporary political rise. Though the situation of Babylonian-Persian Jewry in the thirteenth century was very gloomy,[4] we know that under Arghūn Jews again ventured on the stage of history and took part in the political and economic texture of general affairs. The privileged position of Christians and Jews also expressed itself in a special decree issued by Arghūn, according to which only Christians and Jews, but no Mohammedans, were to be given administrative posts.[5] This attitude afforded Jewry an

[1] Chabot, op. cit., p. 53; Montgomery, p. 151; Budge, p. 165. Montgomery, ibid., remarks on p. 17: " None appears to have been more favourably inclined to Christianity than the Ilkhan Arghūn."

[2] Montgomery, ibid., p. 17: " Had Arghūn, following in the track of statesmanlike popes, won over the West to his plan of a Crusade against the Mamluke power, the centre of Islam's resistance, he might have become the Constantine of his Mongols."

[3] L. Brehier, *L'Église et l'Orient au Moyen Age*, Paris, 1907, p. 258: " jamais aucun moment n'avait paru plus favorable (pour l'église) pour diriger contre le monde musulman une attaque décisive." Montgomery, ibid., p. 11: " militant Christendom missed the greatest opportunity in its history."

[4] On the fate of the Jews of Baghdād at the time of Hūlāgū's conquest cf. Mann, " Une source de l'histoire Juive au xiii siecle," in *REJ.* 1926, vol. 82, particularly p. 373; and the Epistle of Jacob b. Eli from Venice, published in *Jeschurun*, ed. Kobak, 1868, vol. vi, pp. 1–34. According to Bar Hebræus, ed. Budge, p. 418, f. 489, Hūlāgū granted freedom from taxation to all except the Jews. On the internal history of Oriental Jewry at that period cf. S. Poznanski, *Babylonische Gaonim im nachgaonäischen Zeitalter*, Berlin, 1914; S. Assaf, *Iggroth Rabbi Samuel b. Ali*, Jerusalem, 1930 (Hebrew); J. Mann, *Texts and Studies in Jewish History and Literature*, Cincinnatti, 1932; W. Fischel, Arabische Quellen zur Geschichte der babylonischen Judenheit im 13. Jahrhundert, *MGWJ.*, 1935, pp. 302–322.

[5] Cf. Bar Hebræus, p. 485, f. 568, " Governors should never appoint the Arab to be a scribe, but only the Christians and the Jews." Waṣṣāf, fol. 201*a*, also tells of the exclusion of Mohammedans from the administration, and of the prohibition against their appearance in the camp of the Īl-Khān.

unheard-of political opportunity, and alone makes it possible to understand how we come to observe a Sa'd ad-Daula, and with him a definite Jewish group, rising to the topmost rank of public affairs.

Name and Family

Ibn al-Fuwaṭi [1] calls him Sa'd ad-Daula b. aṣ-Ṣafi, the Jewish physician. In Waṣṣāf [2] we meet him as Sa'd ad-Daula b. aṣ-Ṣafi ad-Daula of Abhar. In Rashīd ad-Dīn,[3] Sa'd ad-Daula is the son of Hibatallah b. Muhadhdhib ad-Daula abhari. Ḥamdullah Mustawfi [4] offers us the most detailed pedigree. He speaks of Sa'd ad-Daula b. Ṣafī ad-Daula b. Hibatallah b. Muhadhdhib ad-Daula abhari yahūdi. Bar Hebræus [5] refers to him simply as "the Jew Sa'd ad-Daula", and Abu'l-Fidā',[6] an-Nuwairi,[7] and Mufaḍḍal b. a. Faḍā'il [8] also know only of سعد الدولة اليهودى .

It is remarkable that his actual name is not given in any source. Instead we are given only his title, the name of honour "Sa'd ad-Daula", the "Support of the State". Particularly noteworthy is the fact that according to the genealogy quoted from the sources above, his father, grandfather, and great-grandfather carried the title "ad-Daula" as part of their names. Waṣṣāf's criticism [9] that Sa'd ad-Daula, in conscious imitation of the custom of the Buwayhid dynasty,

[1] *Ibn al-Fuwaṭi*, p. 450; see also p. 454.

[2] Fol. 196*b*. In the superscription to his chapter on Sa'd ad-Daula Waṣṣāf refers to him as Sa'īd ad-Daula سعيد الدولة. But in the text reference is made only to the form سعد. This induced also European scholars to refer to him as Sa'īd ad-Daula. Cf. Howorth, op. cit. Also Ghāzī b. al-Wāsiṭi, fol. 28, has سعيد الدولة.

[3] Fol. 149*a*.

[4] *Ta'rīkh-i-Guzida*, ed. Browne, p. 587.

[5] p. 478, f. 561.

[6] *Annales*, ed. Reiske, iv, 18.

[7] MS. Leiden, fol. 203*a*.

[8] *Histoire*, ed. Blochet, xx, p. 550.

[9] Waṣṣāf, fol. 199*a*.

began to incorporate the designation الدولة in his own and his brothers' names, seems unjustified.[1]

We are not informed that Sa'd ad-Daula had any children. Bar Hebræus, to be sure, does state that Sa'd ad-Daula was the father-in-law of the governor of Baghdād; but this statement is not confirmed by evidence from any other source. On the other hand, the sources mention two of his brothers, Fakhr ad-Daula and Amīn ad-Daula, as well as a cousin, a Tabrīz doctor by the name of Muhadhdhib ad-Daula Abū Manṣūr. A certain Muhadhdhib ad-Daula Naṣr b. al-Māsha'īri was probably a relative as well.[2]

As his birthplace the sources unanimously give Abhar[3] in the Persian province Jibāl, on the road to Kazwīn. Hence during the thirteenth century there must have been a Jewish community in Abhar of which we are so far not informed from Hebrew sources.

According to Abu'l-Fidā',[4] and according to him alone, Sa'd ad-Daula spent his early years in Mosul. Other sources, however, state that he commenced in Baghdād, whence he was finally summoned to the court of Arghūn at Tabrīz.[5] In Tabrīz he also met his death. In any case, the scanty geographical information of the sources make it clear that his seats of personal activity were confined to Baghdād, the centre of 'Irāq, and Tabrīz,[6] the residence of the Īl-Khān and capital of Persia.

[1] On the change in meaning of the laqab دولة cf. Qalqashandi, *Ṣubḥ al-A'shā*, v, pp. 442–3. Cf. E. Blochet (*Patrologia Orientalis*, xx, p. 39). On Jewish bearers of ad-Daula cf. M. Steinschneider, "Introduction to the Arabic Literature," *JQR.*, 1897–1900.

[2] On these names see further below.

[3] Rashīd ad-Dīn, fol. 149*a*; Waṣṣāf, fol. 196*b*; *Mustawfī*, p. 587; an-Nuwairi, MS. Leiden, fol. 203*a*. On Abhar cf. Le Strange, *The Lands of the Eastern Caliphate.*

[4] Ed. Reiske, iv, 18.

[5] Abāqā made Tabrīz the official capital of the Īl-Khān Empire, and the city retained this position among his successors until Uljāytū ascended the throne. Cf. *E.I.*, Art. Tabrīz.

[6] Here we do not note the various summer and winter residences in which Sa'd ad-Daula would occasionally pass his time together with the Īl-Khān.

The year of his birth is not known. The first dependable date supplied by the sources concerning his activities is the year 682/1284, at the beginning of Arghūn's rule. He must have been well known by that time on account of his experience and many-sided knowledge. The last certain date is 1291, the year of his death. During the years between 1284 and 1291 (682–689) is, therefore, to be found the story of his rise and of his career as a statesman, to which we now propose to devote ourselves more closely.

Early Years in Baghdād

Sa'd ad-Daula first appears as a physician, a Jewish doctor,[1] and during the early years of his public career he is always referred to as such. According to an-Nuwairi,[2] Sa'd ad-Daula devoted himself, from the very commencement of his activities, to medicine, which must hence have been his original profession. Abu'l-Fidā',[3] however, reports that in the beginning Sa'd ad-Daula acted in the artisan market at Mosul as an auctioneer (*dallāl*). But in the light of his later career both contradictory statements might be correct, for even in later years Sa'd ad-Daula combined with equal success the art of the great physician and that of the practical administrator and expert financier.

In any case, at first we meet him as a physician in government service at Baghdād.[4] From the sources we learn that, together with his medical practice, he found opportunities of making himself familiar with all fiscal questions at Baghdād; according to Rashīd ad-Dīn [5] he was appointed a member of

[1] *Ibn al-Fuwaṭi*, p. 450, الحكيم اليهودى; in Rashīd ad-Dīn, f. 149*a*, طبيبى.

[2] MS. Leiden, fol. 203*a*: فى اوّل امره يشتغل بالطبّ . . . فتميّز.

[3] Ed. Reiske, iv, 18: ومبدأ امره . . . دلال بسوق الصناعة بالموصل.

[4] Waṣṣāf, fol. 197*a*. *Ibn al-Fuwaṭi*, p. 433, reports that in the year 682 a certain Sa'd ad-Daula b. aṣ-Ṣafi ad-Daula was dismissed from his supervision of the endowment of a Baghdād hospital. Would this be our Sa'd ad-Daula?

[5] Rashīd ad-Dīn, fol. 149*a*.

the Dīwān of the Baghdād administration in the year 1284 as a result of his familiarity with administrative conditions.

His abilities must have aroused the enmity of his superior officials as well as that of his colleagues, for we learn that in order to remove him from Baghdād they lauded his great medical capacities, claiming that as a doctor his equal was not to be found, and that he must therefore be transferred to the Court of Arghūn.[1]

We have no detailed information regarding the collision between Sa'd ad-Daula and his Baghdād opponents. Ibn al-Fuwaṭi tells only of the victory of his foes when he records [2]: "He (Qutlugh Shāh, the Governor of Baghdād) demanded the removal of Sa'd ad-Daula b. aṣ-Ṣafi, the Jewish physician, from him, and that he should withdraw from co-operation in the administration. This was complied with."

This came about in the year 1288, and Sa'd ad-Daula was compelled to exchange Baghdād for Tabrīz, the residence of Arghūn. His banishment to Tabrīz marks a new chapter in his life and his rise to power. Ibn al-Fuwaṭi, usually no more than a dry annalist, indicates later developments with the words: "Through his proximity to the presence of the Sulṭān he attained something that would never have crossed his mind." [3]

At Arghūn's Court in Tabrīz

In Tabrīz Sa'd ad-Daula won the friendship of one of the leading Mongol Emīrs, General Ardūqīa,[4] with whom he remained closely connected until the day of his death. At first Sa'd ad-Daula confined himself to his medical profession

[1] Waṣṣāf, fol. 197*a*; Rashīd ad-Dīn, 149*a*.

[2] *Ibn al-Fuwaṭi*, p. 450.

[3] *Ibn al-Fuwaṭi*, p. 450.

[4] He was an emissary of Arghūn to the Court of Qublai Khān in order to inform the latter of Arghūn's appointment as ruler. He returned to Tabrīz in the same year in which Sa'd ad-Daula was transferred there, and became the military counsellor and friend of the Īl-Khān. Cf. Howorth, p. 320.

at the court.[1] As a physician he came into contact with Arghūn, who began to take his advice to an increasing degree. His great medical capabilities must have induced Arghūn to make him his personal physician. As Waṣṣāf informs us, " when Arghūn became sick Sa'd ad-Daula alone was able to cure him." [2]

It was not, however, the doctor alone, but also the man, who found favour in Arghūn's eyes. Even Waṣṣāf could not avoid pointing out this human side of Sa'd ad-Daula's character, relating that he knew how to demean himself with dukes, was of excellent address, and spoke perfectly both Turkish and Mongolian, which he had learnt during his stay in Baghdād.[2] Hence Arghūn, in his free hours and particularly during convalescent periods, was very fond of chatting with his physician ; and his trust toward the other went so far that Sa'd ad-Daula's advice was gradually called for even in matters of policy and financial administration.[3] On such occasions the early years at Baghdād, during which he had had special opportunities of studying the administration and more particularly financial questions very thoroughly, stood him in good stead.[4] At one such conversation it must have happened, as Ibn al-Fuwaṭi reports, that " Sa'd ad-Daula revealed to him (Arghūn) the situation in 'Irāq, and informed him of all the factors involved ".[5]

It is advisable to pause for a moment in order to consider that situation and those factors.

The Administration of 'Irāq

The administration of Arghūn's empire was in the hands of the Mongol Emīr Būqā, a loyal supporter of Arghūn,

[1] *Ibn al-Fuwaṭi*, p. 450.

[2] Waṣṣāf, fol. 197*a*.

[3] From this developed an uncommonly close friendship between the Mongol ruler and the Persian Jew.

[4] Waṣṣāf, fol. 197*a*, also praises Sa'd ad-Daula's understanding of tax and financial problems.

[5] Loc. cit., p. 450. Waṣṣāf, loc. cit., has a parallel text with more details.

through whom the latter had reached the throne. In gratitude Arghūn gave him high titles of honour and appointed him head of the entire administration of the empire.[1]

This Būqā became the most powerful man in the empire, and according to Bar Hebræus [2] became " so high and mighty in the kingdom that even the princes and the princesses . . . the captains of the armies of the Mongols used to come and submit to him ". At the tide of his power Būqā appointed his brother Arūq chief " of the financial administration of ʿIrāq and Diyār Bekr ",[3] or, in the version of Bar Hebræus, " over all the countries of Babil and Adherbaijān and Beth Naḥrīn." [4]

All sources [5] describe the reign of terror of these two brothers, the oppression of the subject as a result of their extortionate methods of tax collection, and their ruthless enrichment of themselves at the cost of the treasury during their six years of office.[6] " About the affairs of Arghūn they were negligent and they occupied themselves with the collection of riches and horses and gold and silver and treasure," states Bar Hebræus. Ibn al-Fuwaṭi also gives a detailed picture of the mismanagement of ʿIrāq brought about by Arūq and Qutlugh Shāh,[7] the Governor he had appointed over Baghdād. Bad harvests, famine, sickness, high prices, and brigandage weighed heavily on the population. In addition there were unfortunate experiments with the currency, the abolition of the copper coinage and the striking of a new silver coin, frequent changes in the value of the dirham

[1] *Ibn al-Fuwaṭi*, p. 436 : وجعل اليه تدبير ممالكه .

[2] Loc. cit., p. 477, fol. 560.

[3] *Ibn al-Fuwaṭi*, pp. 437 ff.

[4] Loc. cit.

[5] Waṣṣāf, fol. 197*b*, Rashīd ad-Dīn, fol. 149*b*–152*a*, Bar Hebræus, p. 478, f. 560, *Ibn al-Fuwaṭi*, p. 437, give detailed accounts of Būqā and Arūq which do not need to be quoted here.

[6] According to Rashīd ad-Dīn, fol. 149*b*, Arūq annually retained a sum of 500 tōmāns from the taxes for himself.

[7] It was this Qutlugh Shāh who caused Saʿd ad-Daula's transfer to Tabrīz.

(inflation), etc.,[1] and last, but by no means least, the compulsory loans extorted from the merchants.[2]

So great grew dissatisfaction with this regime that, according to Bar Hebræus,[3] three of the notables of Baghdād went to Arghūn and laid a charge against Arūq and his corrupt system. At first Arghūn did not believe the charges and wished to wait until Arūq himself came to the camp. But meanwhile Būqā had the three emissaries murdered in secret; and it seems that this step impelled Arghūn to take action with regard to the many charges and complaints against the two brothers.

It was at this juncture, as it seems, that Sa'd ad-Daula, upon the request of the emperor, revealed the situation in 'Irāq, and began to make a vehement onslaught, based on his own experience in Baghdād, against the system of Būqā, Arūq, and their group. "He began," Ibn al-Fuwaṭi tells us, "with the accusations against the Emīr Būqā and the latter's brother Arūq, and showed him the sources of their (private) income from the State." [4]

This criticism must have worked, for it is stated that "thereupon Arghūn changed his mind with regard to them (Būqā and Arūq)".[5]

2. The Political Rise of Sa'd ad-Daula

The further course of events is not detailed precisely in the sources, but all of them make it clear that Sa'd ad-Daula now stepped out of his role of physician and private adviser to Arghūn and began to take a hand in affairs as a statesman and director of financial policy.

According to Bar Hebræus,[6] Sa'd ad-Daula appeared before

[1] The information to be found in *Ibn al-Fuwaṭi* for the years 682–6, pp. 430–1, 446–7, 449, etc., is very valuable for a monetary history of 'Irāq.

[2] *Ibn al-Fuwaṭi*, p. 451.

[3] p. 478, f. 561.

[4] *Ibn al-Fuwaṭi*, pp. 450, 451.

[5] *Ibn al-Fuwaṭi*, p. 451.

[6] p. 478, f. 561.

Arghūn and said: "If you will stop the going down of Arūq to Baghdād, I myself will bring the double of the revenue which is brought each year to the camp." And straightway the command went forth that Arūq was not to go down to Baghdād again, and he was to have no further command over it. "And the Emīrs handed affairs over to the Jew." The sum which he promised to provide amounted, according to Rashīd ad-Dīn,[1] to 500 tōmāns; and he was immediately set in charge of the financial administration of Baghdād in place of Arūq.

But according to Ibn al-Fuwaṭi, Sa'd ad-Daula's appointment as Governor of Baghdād was preceded by another measure, namely, the sending of a commission of inquiry to that city.

This commission, of which Ardūqīa and Sa'd ad-Daula were members, had as its task the study and examination of all details of the situation on the spot.[2] Upon their arrival they betook themselves to Arūq and immediately demanded from him an explanation of the compulsory loans he had extorted from the citizens. They then called for the accounts and all the money derived from the revenue. After their examination "they returned again together to the Sulṭān, and Sa'd ad-Daula informed him what Arūq and Qutlugh Shāh had done to the subjects and what their own income in money had been. Thereupon he (Arghūn) ordered this to be confiscated from Qutlugh Shāh".[3] In the year 1289 Sa'd ad-Daula and Ardūqīa returned to Baghdād, vested with precise authority and powers. They had the duty of immediately rescinding all firmāns, attestations, and diplomas; and as soon as this was done they declared Qutlugh Shāh to be deposed from his office of Governor of Baghdād by order of the Sulṭān.[4]

[1] Loc. cit., fol. 149*b*.

[2] *Ibn al-Fuwaṭi*, p. 451: لتصفح احوال العراق.

[3] Loc. cit., 451.

[4] *Ibn al-Fuwaṭi*, 454; Waṣṣāf, 197*b*–198*a*.

The deposition of Qutlugh Shāh was the first decisive stroke against the regime of Būqā and Arūq. They felt their position becoming insecure and prepared a conspiracy against Arghūn. The preparations for this conspiracy, which are described in detail,[1] were discovered, and the Īl-Khān ordered "that the Emīr Būqā, his children, and his supporters should be executed as well as his brother the Emīr Arūq, who was in Diyār Bekr".[2] This was done in the year 688/1289.

The end of this regime meant the commencement of Sa'd ad-Daula's political rise, during which he rapidly rose from one position to another.

Upon the successful completion of his duties as member of the commission of inquiry, he was appointed Controller (مشرف) of the Dīwān al-'Irāq[3] and chief of the financial administration of Baghdād and 'Irāq. Upon him devolved the supervision of the entire revenue and taxation system of 'Irāq.[4] With this appointment began his career as statesman.

Almost all sources, and primarily Waṣṣāf, describe the wisdom and justice with which Sa'd ad-Daula performed the duties of his office.[5] He refunded to the citizens the money extorted from them by the compulsory loan, collected the arrears of taxes, balanced the budget,[6] doubled the income from taxation, filled the state treasury and the private treasury of Arghūn, and "achieved success after success from day to day".[7] He even declared that he could have collected still more if the Emīrs had not hindered him.[8]

[1] Rashīd ad-Dīn, fol. 150*b* ff.

[2] *Ibn al-Fuwaṭi*, 457; cf. also Rashīd ad-Dīn, fol. 150*b* ff.

[3] *Ibn al-Fuwaṭi*, 455. In Ghāzi b. al-Wāsiṭī, fol. 28*a*, he is called صاحب ديوان بغداد والعراق.

[4] *Ibn al-Fuwaṭi*, 454.

[5] Waṣṣāf, fol. 197*b*–198*a*. He remarks *inter alia* that the treasure of Arghūn piled up like a mountain.

[6] *Ibn al-Fuwaṭi*, 454.

[7] Rashīd ad-Dīn, fol. 151*a*.

[8] Thereupon Arghūn had these Emīrs executed. Cf. Rashīd ad-Dīn, fol. 151*a*.

Sa'd ad-Daula did not remain مشرف for long. In recognition of his services to the state, Arghūn appointed him in the same year, 1289, Chief of the entire Administration, First Minister, and Vizier over all the countries of his Empire.[1]

The titular description of his post is given variously in the sources. Waṣṣāf[2] describes Sa'd ad-Daula's post and unlimited power with the words سعد الدولة . . . حاكم مال وملك.

Ibn al-Fuwaṭi[3] now calls him صاحب ديوان الممالك and Bar Hebræus says[4]: "The king of kings (Arghūn) ordered that Sa'd ad-Daula, the Jew, hitherto the Governor of Baghdād, should be appointed Chief of the administrative officials, i.e. Sāḥib Dīwān, throughout all provinces of the Empire." According to Abu'l-Fiḍā' he was appointed "over all the lands which were in the hands of the Tatārs".[5] According to Rashīd ad-Dīn[6] he became Vizier. Muṣtawfi[7] also knows him henceforward as Vizier, as do Mufaḍḍal b. abi'l Faḍā'il[8] and others. an-Nuwairi, reviewing the way which led Sa'd ad-Daula from physician to vizier, sums up: "At first he practised medicine and distinguished himself; and he progressed further until he attained the Vizierate."[9]

After his appointment as responsible chief of the administration of the Empire, Sa'd ad-Daula immediately removed all his opponents and filled the posts of most authority in the administration with those upon whom he could depend—Mongols, Muslims, Christians, and Jews, but primarily with members of his own family.

(*a*) As governor of Baghdād or 'Irāq he appointed his

[1] It appears that Ardūqia caused this appointment to be given to Sa'd ad-Daula.

[2] Waṣṣāf, fol. 198*a*.

[3] p. 458.

[4] p. 484, f. 569.

[5] Ed. Reiske, iv, p. 18.

[6] *Rashīd ad-Dīn*, fol. 152*a*–*b*.

[7] Ed. Browne, p. 587.

[8] Ed. Blochet, p. 485.

[9] MS. Leiden, fol. 203*a*.

brother Fakhr ad-Daula,[1] together with Muhadhdhib ad-Daula b. al-Māsha'īri,[2] apparently a relative of his, to whom one Jamāl ad-Dīn ad-Dastajirdāni was appointed secretary.

(*b*) Another brother, Amīn ad-Daula,[3] was set in charge of the district of Mosul and Diyār Bekr, Diyār Rabī'a and Mārdīn[4]; and according to Bar Hebræus a certain Tāj ad-Dīn b. Mukhāṭir was appointed his secretary.[5]

(*c*) In charge of Adherbaijān was set, according to Waṣṣāf,[6] Labīd b. a. Rabī'a, the Jew; Rashīd ad-Dīn mentions that the governor of Tabrīz and district (by which Adherbaijān would be meant) was the Jewish physician Muhadhdhib ad-Daula abū Manṣūr, a relative of Sa'd ad-Daula.[7]

(*d*) According to Rashīd ad-Dīn the governor of Fārs was a certain Shams ad-Daula b. Majd ad-Daula, the astronomer; Waṣṣāf, too, knows him, but does not mention his profession or his father's name.[8]

[1] In *Ibn al-Fuwaṭi*, pp. 458, 464. Similarly in Waṣṣāf, 198*a–b*, *Rashīd ad-Dīn*, fol. 153*a*. Bar Hebræus, loc. cit., who scarcely ever mentions names, says no more than "Arghūn appointed his brother (i.e. of Sa'd ad-Daula) Governor of Baghdād".

[2] This مهذب الدولة نصر بن المشعيرى is mentioned several times in *Ibn al-Fuwaṭi*, pp. 438, 458, 464, 465; cf. also *Rashīd ad-Dīn*, fol. 153*a*; Waṣṣāf, 206*a*. The Dīwān of El'āzār Hababli (*ca.* 1250) also mentions a מהד'ב אלדולה בן אל מאשעירי, who must have been one of the outstanding personalities of Baghdād Jewry. It is unlikely, considering the dates, that he can have been the Muhadhdhib of the Arabic sources. Cf. Poznanski, *Babyl. Geonim*, p. 10, note 5; Mann, *Texts and Studies*, pp. 268, 300, 304; *JQR.*, xii, p. 196.

[3] In *Ibn al-Fuwaṭi*, p. 466, stands امير الدولة, which the editor did not correct, however, to امين الدولة.

[4] *Ibn al-Fuwaṭi*, p. 466, mentions only Mosul as the administrative district of Amīn ad-Daula. *Rashīd ad-Dīn*, fol. 153*a*, speaks only of Diyār Bekr; cf. Waṣṣāf, fol. 198.

[5] Bar Hebræus, p. 484, f. 569.

[6] Fol. 198*b*.

[7] Fol. 153*a*.

[8] Waṣṣāf, fol. 198*b*. There is no need to regard this شمس الدولة as a brother of Sa'd ad-Daula, though he may have been a relative. This Shams ad-Daula is represented by Waṣṣāf in a surprisingly favourable light, cf. fol. 201.

Mention is further made of a certain Najīb ad-Daula as a confidant of Sa'd ad-Daula, who attained political prominence and is probably identical with the oculist known in the sources as Najīb ad-Dīn.[1]

While Sa'd ad-Daula thus transferred the administration of the most important provinces of the Īl-Khān Empire [2] to his brothers and relatives, he himself directed the central administration personally from Tabrīz together with his intimate friend and counsellor Ardūqīa, the Mongol general and Emīr.

His Jewish Consciousness

What is likely to have been the attitude of the large Jewish community [3] in Persia and 'Irāq towards the power and influence of Sa'd ad-Daula and his family ?

They must certainly have been filled with pride that one of their own wielded the greatest power in the State. Their state of mind is probably fairly accurately given by Bar Hebræus when he states that " they were boasting proudly of their

[1] *Rashīd ad-Dīn*, fol. 154*a*. He was sent to Khorāsān in order to aid Arghūn's troops in suppressing the rebellion that had broken out there. This is possibly the source of the accusation brought by Waṣṣāf, fol. 202*a*, that he wished to have 200 of the notables of Khorāsān executed by order of Sa'd ad-Daula. Cf. E. Blochet, *Introduction à l'histoire des Mongols*, p. 22. *Vide* also Zetterstéen, *Beiträge zur Geschichte der Mamlukensultane*, p. 76, 21 : نجيب الكحال اليهودى.

[2] Sa'd ad-Daula could not, however, nominate any of his relatives to responsible positions in the provinces Khorāsān and Rūm. The administration of these provinces was in the hands of relatives of Arghūn.

[3] We have no definite idea of the number of Jews in Persia or Mesopotamia at that period. The reports brought back from their travels by Benjamin of Tudela and by Petakhia of Regensburg are our Jewish sources for the twelfth century. The existence of numerous Jewish communities can be inferred from, among others, the travels of William of Rubruck (1253–5) in *Contemporaries of Marco Polo*, pp. 198–9 : " In the city of Samaron, where there were many Jews, there are other shut-in places where Jews live, but I cannot tell you for certain *though there are many Jews in all the cities of Persia*." In Baghdād, Mosul, Tabrīz, and other large towns there were naturally large Jewish communities.

exaltation and occupied with their power". The social effect of the rise of Sa'd ad-Daula is shown by Bar Hebræus: "Up to the present day no Jew has ever been raised to a position of exalted honour among them; the humbler among them are engaged as tanners or dyers or tailors. But truly the honourable ones and the fortunate among them exalt the art of healing and the art of the scribe, but in situations in which others will not demean themselves to work, they will work." [1]

It is not impossible that the singular rise of Sa'd ad-Daula may have led to the expression of exaggerated hopes and thoughts, and that the Jews regarded him as a deliverer in their hour of need.[2] To be sure, we possess no sources for such a statement on the Jewish side, but find the following suggestive passage in Bar Hebræus: "Therefore many of the Jews who were on the fringes of the world gathered together to him and they all with one mouth said 'Verily by means of this man the Lord hath raised on high the horn of redemption and the hope of glory for the sons of the Hebrews in their last days!'" [3]

It is, of course, a vain effort to try and discover who were meant by the "Jews who were on the fringes of the world". Are only those Jews meant who lived within the Mongol

[1] We have to thank this source for an interesting glimpse of the employments followed by Oriental Jewry. The professional divisions of the Jews had remained fairly stable since the travels of Benjamin of Tudela in the twelfth century. Many dyers, weavers, etc., were still to be found among Jews in the East, as we learn from Bar Hebræus, p. 490, f. 575. Compare the statement regarding Jewish callings in the tenth century made by al-Jāḥiẓ, ed. Finkel. That there were also many wealthy Jews at the time of Arghūn can be seen from the numerous attacks upon and sackings of Jewish houses at that period. The sources also speak quite clearly of large Jewish money treasures. Cf. *Mufaḍḍal b. a. Faḍā'il*, vol. xiv, p. 550, and Zetterstéen, loc. cit., p. 9.

[2] Howorth, *History of the Mongols*, p. 333, says: "Well might the Jews fancy that their Messiah had arrived, where they saw one of their long-despised race treated as an equal by the princes . . . and even by the Ilkhan himself."

[3] p. 490, f. 575.

Empire? Does it include all Oriental Jewry? Or even European Jewry? [1]

Apart from the effect of Sa'd ad-Daula on Jewry, he seems to have had a positive attitude towards Judaism. On account of the lack of contemporary Hebrew documents,[2] to be sure, we do not know how far he devoted or needed to devote himself to Jewish affairs in his capacity as Vizier.[3] But we learn from a number of facts that he possessed a strongly developed Jewish consciousness. Not only is the fact characteristic that he remained a Jew, but also the manner in which his brothers, kinsmen, and coreligionists were borne in mind in filling posts in the administration. According to Waṣṣāf [4] he even strove consciously to raise the prestige of the Jewish people throughout the world. Ghāzi b. al-Wāsiṭī [5]

[1] The Jewish historian Graetz, *Geschichte der Juden*, vol. vii, pp. 188 ff., and Note 10, pp. 419 ff., wishes to connect the Jewish immigration tendency indicated by Bar Hebræus with the emigration movement to Palestine and Asia in general which began at that time from Germany and Western Europe, and under the influence of which the renowned Rabbi Mēīr of Rothenburg prepared to take the wanderer's staff in hand. See also Zimmels, *Beitraege zur Geschichte der Juden in Deutschland im* 13 *Jahrhundert*, Wien, 1926, p. 4, and L. Baeck, *Rabbi Meir aus Rothenburg*, Frankfurt-am-Main, 1895. Nonetheless, no source worthy of the name has yet been produced to show that the news of Sa'd ad-Daula's rise had reached Europe at that period.

[2] Although it has not yet been possible to find reference to Sa'd ad-Daula in any Hebrew source, various attempts have been made to identify him with one or other "exalted person" of the thirteenth century on the basis of a Hebrew Geniza fragment. Graetz, loc. cit., identifies a certain Mordekhai b. al-Kharabīya with him; but the assumption that Sa'd ad-Daula was named Mordekhai has no grounds. The investigations of Israel Lévi, "Le tombeau de Mardochée et d'Esther," *REJ.*, Paris, 1898, vol. 36, pp. 237–255, are based on this identification by Graetz. Poznanski, *Babyl. Geonim*, p. 9, also discards this identification. Cf. Steinschneider, *JQR.* xii, p. 129. There are also no grounds for A. Marmorstein's attempt (*Jewish Guardian*, London, 9th August, 1929, pp. 7–8) to identify Sa'd ad-Daula with a Baghdād Exilarch.

[3] It seems that there were no relations between Sa'd ad-Daula and the contemporary leaders of the Mesopotamian Jewish community, the Exilarch David b. Daniel of Mosul or the Gaon Samuel b. Daniel ha-Kohen of Baghdād; cf. Poznanski, *Babyl. Geonim*, pp. 121–2.

[4] Waṣṣāf, fol. 198*b*.

[5] Ed. Gottheil, p. 410, fol. 28*a*–*b*.

also says that he was striving to elevate the status of the Jews and to raise their condition (رفع منار اليهود).

The following anecdote, reported by Ibn al-Fuwaṭi, is particularly interesting: "Sa'd ad-Daula betook himself to a height on which stood the mausoleum of Mūsā b. Ja'far; he visited his grave and took a copy of the Qur'ān in order to seek for a good omen.[1] And he struck upon the verse, 'O you Children of Israel, we rescued you from your foe and set you upon the right side of the mountain and sent the manna and the quail to fall for you.'[2] Thereupon he rejoiced and distributed a hundred dīnārs to the 'Alids and the people."[3] This "thereupon he rejoiced" is characteristic, and permits certain conclusions to be drawn as to his Jewish feelings.[4]

Recognition and Criticism

His activities as Vizier and responsible director of the affairs of the Empire are highly praised in all sources,[5] and even Waṣṣāf says in his honour that Sa'd ad-Daula established the administration on the bases of law and justice, that his reforms led to the disappearance of oppression, robbery, and thieving, that the finances of the state were consolidated and that all the inhabitants benefited from his successful efforts.[6]

[1] It was a common custom at that period to seek for a "sign" before important decisions or events. The use of a copy of the Qur'ān and the visit to a Muslim grave show the influence of his surroundings.

[2] *Sūra*, 20, 82.

[3] *Ibn al-Fuwaṭi*, p. 457.

[4] Was it possibly in connection with this stichomancy from the Qur'ān that Sa'd ad-Daula felt himself called upon to free his own community, the Jews, from their foes? It is impossible to do more than ask whether Sa'd ad-Daula furthered the great scheme of Abāqā and Arghūn for freeing the Holy Land from the Mamelūks by a joint Mongol-Christian Crusade. In any case, Arghūn's plan could easily have meant an opportunity for Jewry at that period, too.

[5] Rashīd ad-Dīn and Ibn al-Fuwaṭi give very few details of Sa'd ad-Daula's internal policy. Waṣṣāf is more informative.

[6] Waṣṣāf, fol. 198*b*–200*b*, gives the text of the decree revising the judicial system (fol. 198*b*), as well as the decree concerning the security and facilitation of the pilgrimage to Mecca (fol. 200*a*). Sa'd ad-Daula also

Arghūn's trust in him grew and transformed itself into an ever closer friendship, regarding which the sources offer certain information.[1] Bar Hebræus declares: "This Jew triumphed in every way and attained the greatest glory and honour possible in the time of Arghūn, the king of kings. He alone brought all his political matters to a successful issue and much else besides." [2]

The recognition of Sa'd ad-Daula's deeds also found its expression in verses and poems which represent the "public opinion" of the period. "Arabic and Persian poets . . . and the orators of the age praised him," Waṣṣāf [3] informs us, "and wrote many books concerning his deeds." He himself promoted the sciences and the art of poetry, and not alone by distributing large sums to scholars and poets [4] but also by writing essays and poems which were published in book form. This book had, however, become so rare as early as the time of Waṣṣāf that the latter found it necessary to remark: "There is a copy in Baghdād." [5]

There was, however, another side to the medal. Though there might be nothing to complain against in Sa'd ad-Daula's personality and activities, the fact that he was a Jew left the way open for vehement criticism. Bar Hebræus [6] already cried out: "Behold at the present day there is a Jew governor

ordered that all letters should be dated (fol. 200*b*). Howorth, *History of the Mongols*, iii, p. 333; Weil, *Geschichte der Chalifen*, iv, pp. 148 ff., give details of the measures and reforms of Sa'd ad-Daula according to Waṣṣāf.

[1] When Arghūn was once playing *nerd* with Sa'd ad-Daula the latter permitted himself to cross his legs, which was a breach of manners. But Arghūn paid no attention (Waṣṣāf, fol. 199*b*). In their leisure intervals they always used to converse together at length. When a high official complained to Arghūn of the priority afforded Sa'd ad-Daula, Arghūn had him executed (*Rashīd ad-Dīn*, fol. 153*a*).

[2] p. 490, fol. 575.

[3] Fol. 199*a*.

[4] Doubtless Sa'd ad-Daula, as was generally the custom, had his own house or court poet who flattered him; the amount of the flattery was not independent of the scale of his salary.

[5] Waṣṣāf, fol. 199*a*, gives a few extracts from it. What an excellent historical source it would be if this collection were to be discovered one day!

[6] p. 478, fol. 561.

and general director on the throne of the house of 'Abbās. Observe how Islam has been brought low. . . ." And he adds: "And they (the Muslims) neither cease nor rest from their wickedness and their tyranny."

The appointment of a Jew as the Vizier of a heathen ruler, over a region that was preponderantly Muslim, was a paradoxical situation which was sure to evoke the greatest discontent primarily in the Muslim population. But if Bar Hebræus laments the influence of the Jews in the Īl-Khān Empire of Arghūn, and states that "the man who could confer a favour or benefit or could do harm was never seen at the gate of the kingdom unless he was a Jew",[1] the Christian historian contradicts not only historical fact but even his own accounts. For the privileged position of the Christians in the Mongol Empire equally roused the ire of the Arabs, and he himself reports: "Thus the hatred and ill will of the Arabs towards the Christians grew stronger."[2]

Islamic reactions to Jewish power expressed themselves in all kinds of diatribes, satirical poems, and libels which have found a partial echo in our sources. Thus we learn the following from Ibn al-Fuwaṭi[3]: "In the year 689/1291 a document was prepared in Baghdād by respected individuals which contained libels against Sa'd ad-Daula, together with verses from the Qur'ān and the history of the prophets, that stated the Jews to be a people whom Allah hath debased, and that he who would undertake to raise them would himself be made low by God. Sa'd ad-Daula received information of this and when he acquired a copy he took it and set it before the Sulṭān Arghūn. The latter condemned each individual who had participated therein."

The kind of libel contained in these documents is not stated by Ibn al-Fuwaṭi. But we can find far more in Waṣṣāf, who

[1] p. 490, fol. 575.

[2] Bar Hebræus himself reports that the Muslims objected to administrative posts being filled by both Jews *and* Christians. See p. 489, fol. 574.

[3] *Ibn al-Fuwaṭi*, p. 461.

empties the vials of his hatred on the Jew Sa'd ad-Daula and brings the most impossible accusations against him.

Thus Sa'd ad-Daula is claimed to have advised Arghūn to convert the Ka'ba to a heathen temple,[1] to have proposed to attack Mecca with a fleet, for which purpose he cut down trees in Baghdād, dating from the days of the 'Abbāsids in order to build ships of them.[2] Further, it is reported that he sent his co-religionist, Najīb ad-Dīn, to Khorāsān with a black list of 200 prominent individuals to be slain. He is also stated to have sent a list of seventeen people for execution to Shams ad-Daula at Shīrāz.[3]

Waṣṣāf cannot bring too many charges against Sa'd ad-Daula, and it is with satisfaction that he quotes in his account satirical verses by a poet in order to show how far the public dissatisfaction with "Jewish Domination" went. He used the poem already referred to above in connection with Abū Sa'd b. Sahl at-Tustari, "The Jews of this our time a rank attain," etc., and after the line "Turn Jews, for heaven itself hath turned a Jew", he added the following :—

"Yet wait and ye shall hear their torments cry
And see them fall and perish presently."[4]

3. Downfall and End of Sa'd ad-Daula

The incitements against "Jewish domination" also provided the atmosphere for actual attempts on the lives of Jewish officials in the Mongol Empire. Thus we hear of a

[1] Waṣṣāf, fol. 202*a*. E. Blochet writes in a letter to me (8/7/34) : "Quant à ce que racontre Waṣṣāf que ce fut Sa'd ad-Daula qui propose a Arghoun de remplacer l'Islam par le culte des idoles, c'est une absurdité ; l'idée de substituer le buddhisme à l'Islamisme ne pouvait germer que dans l'idée d'un buddhiste et non d'un juif."

[2] Waṣṣāf, fol. 201*a–b*, also reports a conversation in which Sa'd ad-Daula expounded a new theory of prophecy and the reform of religion, describing Arghūn as a prophet.

[3] Waṣṣāf, fol. 202*a*.

[4] The verses quoted by Waṣṣāf, fol. 202*a*, are identical, with the exception of slight changes, with those quoted from *Ibn Muyassar* on p. 2 above, where the name of the author is given.

conspiracy: "And in those days certain men of the Ishmaelites disguised as merchants were sent to Mosul so that they might leap upon the Emīrs and commanders who were therein and kill them and that a Christian and a Jew might no longer rule in the place. And if they could not leap upon them, they were to kill secretly and craftily." The conspiracy was discovered and the conspirators made the following declaration to Amīn ad-Daula, the Governor of Mosul: "We three men have come to kill you, and three other men have gone to Babil to kill the Jew who is there (Fakhr ad-Daula), and three others have gone to the camp (Tabrīz) to kill the Ṣāḥib Dīwān (Sa'd ad-Daula) who is there." [1]

But certain individuals also on the Mongol side began working against Sa'd ad-Daula. To be sure, the Mongols, who were tolerant in all religious matters, could not see anything actually wrong in the elevation of a Jew as such to the highest posts of the administration. For them there was, as Bar Hebræus states, no difference between Jew, Christian, or heathen. "All they demand is strenuous service and submission." [2] Sa'd ad-Daula, however, had personal enemies among the most influential of the Mongol dukes, first and foremost in the Emīr Tughān, who felt himself ignored as a result of Sa'd ad-Daula's power and Arghūn's unlimited faith in him; he also found himself insulted by the other's proud behaviour.[3] This Tughān is described as the soul of the Mongol opposition to Sa'd ad-Daula, and Waṣṣāf shows how he attempted to poison the atmosphere round Sa'd ad-Daula by court intrigues, and won more and more supporters to his plan of a conspiracy against Sa'd ad-Daula. Through this Tughān and his group the hope for a speedy

[1] p. 489, fol. 574.

[2] p. 484, f. 569.

[3] Rashīd ad-Dīn, fol. 155*b*; Bar Hebræus, p. 490, f. 575: "To the nobles of the camp he paid no heed and he reduced the taking and giving of their lands; he treated with contempt the principal amirs and the directors of general affairs."

collapse of the Jew Sa'd ad-Daula, expressed by the Arab poet, was realized far sooner than expected.

The Īl-Khān Arghūn suddenly became dangerously ill at Tabrīz, and this awakened hopes of a speedy downfall of the Vizier. Arghūn's sickness [1] and the course it followed are described in the sources with as much detail as the efforts made to cure him.[2] That Sa'd ad-Daula as friend and physician did everything he possibly could to heal the sick emperor is particularly stressed. "And the wretched Jew was perplexed by his illness, and with great care he endeavoured in every way possible to heal him," says Bar Hebræus.[3] He was very much shaken, "like a ship upon a stormy sea" and immediately recognized the gravity of the situation knowing that Arghūn's death would signal his own.

As chief of the government he immediately ordered that alms and gifts should be distributed to the poor; he himself expended great sums. But all this and much more could not avail to avert Destiny. Arghūn improved in no way. In the desperate situation in which court circles found themselves, a scapegoat was looked for. At first the cause of the disease [4] was ascribed to the evil eye, to a kind of magic, to women [5]; but finally the circles inimical to Sa'd ad-Daula succeeded in shifting the blame on to his shoulders. Bar Hebræus reports: "Then the Emīrs and the nobles of the camp who despised the Jew, having utterly lost all hope of saving the life of Arghūn, believed as if the Jew himself,

[1] Bar Hebræus, loc. cit., calls Arghūn's sickness an attack of paralysis. According to Waṣṣāf, fol. 203*a*, Arghūn's face became completely yellow.

[2] Rashīd ad-Dīn, fol. 155*a*, also mentions the Mongol Bakhshiān as physician and a certain Amīn ad-Daula.

[3] Bar Hebræus, loc. cit. Only Sa'd ad-Daula and the Emīr Jūshi had access to Arghūn during his sickness (Waṣṣāf, 204*a*). According to Rashīd ad-Dīn, fol. 155, Ardūqīa and Kujjān as well.

[4] Waṣṣāf, fol. 203*a*. According to Rashīd ad-Dīn, fol. 155*a*, the cause of the sickness was a special kind of medicine which Arghūn demanded from his physician Bakhshiān to lengthen his life. He is said to have taken this medicine for eight months.

[5] Rashīd ad-Dīn, fol. 155. Many of the women of his harem are said to have been slain. Cf. also Waṣṣāf, fol. 203*b*.

through the evil of his machinations, was the cause of the sickness of Arghūn." [1]

Although the accusation was an obvious absurdity, since Sa'd ad-Daula must have known that Arghūn's end would lead to his own downfall, it served his enemies at the court as an excuse to get rid of him. At a banquet arranged by Tughān, Sa'd ad-Daula and the majority of his supporters were arrested by the conspirators, a large number of them slain at once, and Sa'd ad-Daula, together with Ardūqīa,[2] executed the following day, the end of the month Safar, 1291, in the house of the Mongol Emīr Tughārjār, two years after his rise to the highest rank of the State.[3]

Arghūn did not learn of the fate of his vizier and friend, although, as Waṣṣāf states, he made inquiries when he noticed Sa'd ad-Daula's absence from his bedside.[4] But he himself died scarcely two weeks after the murder of Sa'd ad-Daula.[5]

[1] Ghāzi b. al-Wāsiṭī, fol. 28*b*, has the following: "Then Sa'id (ad-Daula) struck at Arghūn and plotted against him with some one who gave him poison, after he had impounded the wealth of Islam. . . ." Also in *Mufaḍḍal b. a. Faḍā'il*, 1920, p. 550, we read that the Mongols accused the Jews of having poisoned Arghūn; cf. also *Zettersteen*, p. 9. E. Blochet (ed. Muf. b. a. F.) remarks that Arghūn was not poisoned but died "par une drague qu'un scramana lui faisait prendre pour l'aurita."

[2] Rashīd ad-Dīn, fol. 156*a*. Cf. also Waṣṣāf, fol. 204*a*. Many of the Mongol leaders then went to the house of Sa'd ad-Daula (in Tabrīz). The murder of Sa'd ad-Daula by the Mongol Emīr Tughārjār is reported in detail in an Arabic poem by the Baghdād preacher Zain ad-Dīn 'Ali b. Sa'īd, which is quoted in full by Waṣṣāf (fol. 205*b*). Here we quote a few lines from the English translation of E. G. Browne, given in *Persian Literature under the Tartars*, pp. 34–6:—

> "Tughachar prince, fulfilled with strength and zeal,
> Hath caused the pillars of their power to reel.
> His fleshing falchion on their flesh did feed
> And none would hold him guilty for the deed."

[3] Bar Hebræus, loc. cit., says: "The whole period during which the Jew was director and governor was two years more or less." Cf. also Waṣṣāf, fol. 199*a*.

[4] Fol. 204*b*.

[5] The sources are practically unanimous in reporting Arghūn's death on Rabī'a I, 690 (10/3/1291). According to *Mufaḍḍal b. abi'l-Faḍā'il*, p. 550, the death of Arghūn took place before the murder of Sa'd ad-Daula.

The Catastrophe of Babylonian-Persian Jewry

The sources at our disposal inform us that the murder of Sa'd ad-Daula provided a signal for the Muslims and the Mongols to commence a general attack on the Jewry of the entire Īl-Khān Empire. "Because of him (Sa'd ad-Daula) the Jews throughout the world were hated and ill-treated," remarks Bar Hebræus.[1] First of all the brothers and relatives of Sa'd ad-Daula who served as governors of the various provinces suffered the same fate as he did. Fakhr ad-Daula, the governor of Baghdād, was arrested and slain, and his colleague in the administration of 'Irāq, Muhadhdhib ad-Daula b. Māsha'īri, was captured in Wāsiṭ and later killed in a terrible fashion in Baghdād.[2] The sources note that both chiefs of the administration of 'Irāq met their deaths at the hands of their former secretary, Jamāl ad-Dīn ad-Dastajirdāni. After the downfall of Sa'd ad-Daula the administration of Irāq passed temporarily into the hands of this Jamāl ad-Dīn, and he, incited by others,[3] carried out the bloody sentence.

But *Ibn al-Fuwaṭi*, p. 464, states definitely that the Emīrs slew Sa'd ad-Daula before the death of Arghūn: وان الامراء قتلوا سعد الدولة قبل وفاة السلطان. See also adh-Dhahabi, *Ta'rīkh ad-Duwal*, ii, p. 149; *Abū'l Fidā'*, iv, 27.

[1] *Bar Hebræus*, p. 491, fol. 576. Cf. also the following remark: "Now said they, when this Jew became great and exalted he commanded that a palace should be built for him in Tabrīz, and he buried many pots filled with gold and silver in the walls thereof. Now this fact only became known at that moment, for it was only when the Mongols were torturing them that they showed the places where the pots were; so they dug in the walls and brought them out."

[2] *Ibn al-Fuwaṭi*, p. 465, describes the horrible fashion in which Muhadhdhib ad-Daula met his end. He was sent to Baghdād in iron chains, first brought before Jamāl ad-Dīn for a hearing and asked about hidden treasures. "As concerns the money of the Dīwān it is in the Treasury of the State; but as concerns my own, you know full well that I have no money hidden," replied Muhadhdhib. Thereupon he was set on the rack, dragged through the streets of Baghdād, quartered, burnt, etc. A young Baghdād Jew named *Ibn Fulāla* ابن فلالة met a similar end. Regarding him we possess only the information in *Ibn al-Fuwaṭi*, pp. 465–6.

[3] Fakhr ad-Dīn Muẓaffar b. Ṭarāḥ is said to have incited Jamāl ad-Dīn by saying: "Haste thou to slay him ere he slay thee" عجل بقتل المهذّب

Sa'd ad-Daula's brother in Mosul, Amīn ad-Daula, was also arrested and the same fate was meted out to him as to his brother Fakhr ad-Daula.[1]

The sources report chiefly concerning Baghdād, which was the seat of the greatest Jewish community at that period. Thus we learn: "Then in Babel, when the report of the murder of this Jew was heard, the Arabs armed themselves and went to the quarter of the Jews, because the Jews were all living together in one quarter [2] in Babel. And when they wanted to go in and plunder them, the Jews rose up against them in great strength and they fought against the Arabs and killed and were killed. . . ."

Thanks to the active resistance which the Jews showed to their assailants, as the sources tell, the number of casualties on their side appears to have been small. We learn, however, that as a result of the riot "in Baghdād more than a hundred of the noble and wealthy Jews were slain and their property plundered." [3]

Ibn al-Fuwaṭi [4] also states of the Baghdād attack that "the masses of Baghdād stormed the house of Fakhr ad-Daula and the dwellings of the Jews all together, and took their treasures away". This lasted three days. But although the police took steps against the masses and fought with them, "a section of the crowd spread the report that the governors had permitted the rioting. Thereupon the evildoers and the criminal and the crafty hastened and plundered their dwellings and their shops."

قبل ان يقتلك. Both *Ibn al-Fuwaṭi*, p. 466, and Waṣṣāf, fol. 206*a*, mention these words—an interesting example of their use of identical sources.

[1] *Ibn al-Fuwaṭi*, p. 466 : واعتمد معه [امين الدولة] مثل ما اعتمد مع اخيه فخر الدولة. In Mosul there were attacks by Kurds and Turkomāns for a time on both Jews and Arabs. Cf. *Bar Hebræus*, p. 476, fol. 558.

[2] It is interesting to learn from this passage that the Baghdād Jews lived in a ghetto. This was also presumably the case with other Jewish communities. *Bar Hebræus*, p. 476, fol. 558, refers to the Jewish quarter in Mosul.

[3] Waṣṣāf, fol. 205*b*.

[4] *Ibn al-Fuwaṭi*, pp. 464–6, gives further details.

That the attacks were not limited to Baghdād is shown by Bar Hebræus's report[1]: "Then God stirred up his wrath against the Jews who were in every place. This Sa'd ad-Daula, the Ṣāḥib Dīwān, they killed there (Tabrīz). And with great care the Amirs and nobles sent ambassadors into all the countries which were under the domain of the Mongols, and they seized his brethren and his kinsfolk and they bound them with chains and they plundered their stores of food and they took their sons and their daughters and their slaves, their hand-maidens and their flocks and herds and all their possessions. And he who was killed by them was killed, and those who were left alive returned to their original stations."

"Throughout the lands of Islam," similarly says Waṣṣāf,[2] "the Jewish people were oppressed and their goods plundered," and also Ibn al-Fuwaṭi[3] informs us that "there was no town left in 'Irāq in which the Jews were not served with that which had happened to them in Baghdād, until a part of them embraced Islam, although they later turned back again." Even if it seems to be exaggeration on the part of Mufaḍḍal b. abi'l Faḍā'il[4] to say that "the Mongols turned against all the Jews and slew them to the last man and plundered all their wealth—and they possessed large fortunes"—a tremendous wave of suffering and persecution must have overwhelmed the entire Jewry of 'Irāq and Persia. Even Bar Hebræus was so affected by the calamity that befell the Jews that he had to note: "The trials and wrath which were stirred up against the Jews at this time neither tongue can utter nor the pen write down."[5]

[1] *Bar Hebræus*, loc. cit.

[2] Waṣṣāf, fol. 205*b*.

[3] *Ibn al-Fuwaṭi*, p. 466.

[4] Ed. Blochet, xx, p. 550.

[5] *Bar Hebræus*, loc. cit. The Muslims, however, gave expression to their joy at the end of Jewish domination in many verses filled with enmity against the Jews. Cf. Waṣṣāf, fol. 206 ff. Some of these were published and translated by E. G. Browne, *Persian Literature*, iii, pp. 34–5.

II. Rashīd ad-Daula

The Jews under the Īl-Khāns after Arghūn

The accounts of the persecution of Jewry throughout the Mongol Empire might lead us to suppose that the Jewish question had been radically settled once for all through brute force, and that Jewish influence on public affairs was at an end. But the historical reality was otherwise. To be sure, the "Jewish domination",[1] as Waṣṣāf calls it, was broken and Jewry was flung into the lowest pit of depression. But since the spiritual foundations of the Īl-Khān rule remained unchanged after Arghūn's death, the attitude toward the Jews, once the storm had subsided, became normal again. The tensity of the situation was undoubtedly reduced by the successor of Arghūn, Gaykhātū (1291/1295), whose first step, after his accession to the throne, was the ordering of an investigation so as to bring to justice those guilty of the murder of Sa'd ad-Daula and his adherents.[2]

Sa'd ad-Daula, the sources tell us, was succeeded by a Muslim, Ṣadr ad-Dīn Aḥmad ar-Razzāq, to whom was transferred the direction of affairs of state. He now became صاحب ديوان الممالك.[3] But his first year of office proved him incapable of maintaining the firmly established and truly model financial administration of Sa'd ad-Daula. As a result of the continuous decrease in revenue from taxes, he was compelled in 693/1294 to take the step, remarkable enough for that period of issuing paper money, the so-called "chao" (چاو).

[1] In the margin of the MS. of Waṣṣāf which we have used there are phrases such as تزلزل دولت يهود, اذلال قوم يهود.

[2] Howorth, *History of the Mongols*, iii, p. 360. Gaykhātū himself was present at the first session of the Court. The verdict was that Tughārjār and Kumjukbāl were responsible for the plot as being the originators. But they were mildly treated and later pardoned.

[3] *Ibn al-Fuwaṭi*, p. 474.

The sources give us full information regarding this reform.[1] Thus we read how " the Ṣāḥib Dīwān promulgated a royal command that men should no longer use gold and silver. And he made slips of paper from papyrus which could be written upon and he stamped them with a mark in red and he wrote on them and showed which was for one dīnār, which for two or three . . . and so on up to ten dīnārs. And he called them ' chao ' and the heralds proclaimed throughout the city : ' Whosoever buyeth and selleth and taketh and giveth without using chao shall die the death. And whosoever hath in his hand silver and doth not carry it to the offices of the Government to be stamped therein with the word " chao " and giveth it up and taketh in exchange chao, shall die the death.' And then men remained in a state of great tribulation and indescribable difficulty for a space of two months. For men would not consent to use the contemptible slips of money and they clung to the use of money. And the people cried out against the Ṣāḥib Dīwān. . . . For during these two months the merchants could not trade and the roads were cut and the khans were closed and buying and selling ceased." [2]

This step led the Empire's finances to the brink of destruction, causing a tremendous economic upheaval, which was increased by the long-continued shortage of foodstuffs—a shortage felt even at the Court of Gaykhātū.

It must have been in this critical situation that Gaykhātū, to our astonishment, called in the aid of a Jew. Remarkable as it may seem, only two years after the downfall of Sa'd ad-Daula, *a Jew named Rashīd ad-Daula* was again summoned to the Court of the Īl-Khān in Tabrīz.

The chronicle of Bar Hebræus gives us information concerning this Jew and his special mission. " Now a certain Jew whose name was *Rashīd ad-Daula* had been appointed to prepare food which was suitable for Gaikhatu of every kind

[1] *Ibn al-Fuwaṭi*, p. 477. He says that only those received bread and victuals who accepted the paper money. For further details see Waṣṣāf, Bar Hebræus, and others. Howorth, loc. cit., pp. 370 ff., 392 ff.

[2] *Bar Hebræus*, p. 496, f. 583.

which might be demanded. . . . And thus the Jew stood up strongly in his matter and he spent a large sum of his own money and he bought myriads of sheep and oxen and he appointed butchers and cooks and he was ready in a most wonderful fashion on the condition that in every month of days silver and money should be collected for the Sāḥib Dīwān because the Treasury was empty and it was destitute of money and not even the smallest coin was to be found therein. And he wrote letters and sent to the various countries, but the Jew was unable to collect anything. And thus the whole of his possessions came to an end and as he was unable to stand in a work such as he was doing—he left and fled." [1]

As can be inferred from the duty entrusted to Rashīd ad-Daula, he was a physician by profession, to whom the duty of supervising the commissariat of the Īl-Khān could be entrusted. It is probable that under Abāqā and Arghūn he had already established a reputation as physician and possibly as administrator. In any case, the Jew Rashīd ad-Daula was summoned at a highly critical juncture to deal with a grave situation. However, after great but fruitless efforts he was compelled to drop his public career once again.

Under Ghāzān (1295–1304), the successor of Gaykhātū, it was no longer possible for a Jew to hold a prominent position at the Court. It was Ghāzān who finally broke with the heathen past of his forefathers and with all idea of a Christian-Mongolian Crusade, and became a Muslim.[2] This step, with all its effect on world history, meant the triumph of Islam in Asia over Mongolian paganism as well as over Oriental Christianity.[3] This also caused the Jewish

[1] *Bar Hebræus*, loc. cit.

[2] Cf. the chapter ذكر اسلام غازان in Zetterstéen, *Beiträge*, pp. 34 ff.

[3] It is an interesting historical coincidence that the year 1291, which sealed the fate of Oriental Jewry as a result of the downfall of Sa'd ad-Daula, also saw the end of Christian domination in Palestine and Syria as a result of the fall of Acre. In the Arabic *Beiträge zur Geschichte der Mamlukensultane*, edited by Zetterstéen, p. 5, we find a Qasīda on the fall of Acre which recurs also in *Ibn al-Fuwaṭi*, p. 470. Here the source speaks of دولة الصلب, while Waṣṣāf refers to دولة اليهود.

problem to take on a new aspect. The concept of the *ahl adh-Dhimma* once again became a basic fact in the administration of the state, and it is characteristic that under Ghāzān and his successor Uljāytū (1305–1316) we hear of renewed enactments against the *ahl adh-Dhimma* and of sumptuary laws,[1] as well as of the destruction of synagogues and churches [2] and of the persecution of Christians and Jews.[3]

In such an atmosphere there was naturally no place for any Jew in a prominent position; and for centuries thereafter, in fact, we meet with no more leading Jews who continued to profess Judaism.[4]

[1] Cf. Mustawfī, *Ta'rīkh-i-Guzīda*, p. 595, and other Persian sources. See also *Ibn al-Fuwaṭi*, p. 483. Bar Hebræus reports, p. 507, f. 596: "And he (the commander of Ghāzān) issued a command that the churches and the houses of images and the synagogues of the Jews should be destroyed and that the priests . . . should be treated with ignominy and that tribute and taxes should be imposed upon them. And no Christian was to be seen unless he had a girdle round his loins and no Jew was to be seen in the streets unless he had a mark on his head . . ."

[2] The persecutions of Jews and Christians under Ghāzān and Uljāytū found also an echo in Egypt. Cf. Sa'īd b. Ḥasan, كتاب مسالك النظر p. 357. Further, it is a remarkable coincidence that at the same time, the commencement of the fourteenth century, a sharp reaction set in against the *ahl adh-Dhimma* in the Mamelūk Empire of Egypt and Syria, and the old sumptuary laws and limitations with regard to Government service were once more enforced. Cf. Abu'l-Fidā', *Annales*, iv, p. 47; adh-Dhahabi, *Ta'rīkh ad-Duwal*, ii, 159; Zetterstéen, *Beiträge*, pp. 84 ff. and other sources.

[3] Under Uljāytū Khān (1305–1316), Ghāzān's successor, the position of Jews and Christians only grew worse. The Jews in particular must have been placed under considerable pressure, for at this period we hear of many conversions to Islam. Jewry's complete loss of influence is clearly shown by the fact that it was possible for Uljāytū to deprive the Jews of their rights to the reputed tomb of the prophet Ezekhiel (Dhu'l Kifl), to which shrine the Jews made their annual pilgrimage. The guardianship of this tomb was taken out of Jewish hands, entrusting it to Muslims and building over it a mosque with a minaret. Cf. Mustawfī, *Ta'rīkh*, p. 61; Mustawfī, *Nuzhat al-Qulūb*, ed. Le Strange, pp. 32–3 (parallel version); E. Herzfeld, Einige Buecherschaetze in Persien (*Ephemer. Orient.*, ed. Harrassowitz, January, 1926); D. L. Sassoon, History of the Jews in Basra, *JQR.*, 1927. Cf. J. Obermeyer, *Die Landschaft Babylonien*, Frankfurt-M., 1929, pp. 321 ff.

[4] With Ottoman domination Jews again began to play an influential part. This subject will be treated in a separate paper.

Yet it is under Ghāzān and his immediate successors Uljāytū and Abū Sa'īd, all of them Muslims, that the Jewish question flickered up again in a special form. The vizier of these three Īl-Khāns was a Rashīd ad-Dīn, who was equally physician, historian, and statesman, "the greatest vizier of the Īl-Khān dynasty and one of the greatest men the East has produced." [1] There has been a very lively discussion regarding the presumably *Jewish origin of this vizier.* The standard works of E. Quatremère [2] and E. Blochet [3] have shown, as a result of extensive research in the sources, that the question of Rashīd ad-Dīn's Jewish origin was a very topical one in his time, causing Court circles much discussion. In fact, Rashīd ad-Dīn's familiarity with Jewish religious usages,[4] his knowledge of the Hebrew language and writing,[5] the number of Jews or one-time Jews surrounding him as collaborators, friends, and officials,[6] is highly surprising and

[1] Howorth, loc. cit., iii, p. 589.

[2] E. Quatremère, *Histoire des Mongols de la Perse par Rachid el Din,* publiée, traduite en Français, Paris, 1836.

[3] E. Blochet, *Introduction à l'histoire des Mongols* (Gibb Mem. Vol. xii, London, 1910). See also E. G. Browne, *Persian Literature under Tartar Dominion*, Cambridge, 1920.

[4] According to al-Kashāni (cf. Blochet, p. 19) it was Rashīd ad-Dīn who, at this period of numerous conversions to Islam, introduced the following test of the new converts. They were given a dish of camel-flesh prepared in sour milk which served as a dependable test of their belief in their newly chosen faith, for, as Rashīd ad-Dīn pointed out, according to Mosaic law (Exodus xxxiv, 26) it is forbidden to eat either camel-flesh or meat cooked in milk. Blochet says, loc. cit., p. 29 : "Cette connaissance d'une minutie de la loi mosaïque est bien improbable chez un Musulman de pure race. . . ."

[5] Quatremère, op. cit., pp. lx–lxi, has proved from a number of details in Rashīd ad-Dīn's works that the latter knew Hebrew. In the Court intrigues concerning him a forged Hebrew letter also played a certain part ; his enemies wished to ascribe its authorship to him. Hence he was thought to know Hebrew. This is certainly worthy of remark, and here, too, Blochet observes, ibid., p. 30, "personne n'admettra qu'au commencement du xiv. siècle on ait pu attribuer une lettre écrite en hébreu ou au moins en caractères hébraïques à une personne qui ne fût point juive ou tout au moins d'origine israélite."

[6] We hear much of Jews and former Jews in the immediate circle of Rashīd ad-Dīn. "Le soin que Rachid mettait a chercher ses complices parmi les juifs," says Blochet, p. 29, "semblerait prouver que le vizier appartenait au moins par ses origines à la religion israélite."

does support the assumption of Blochet that Rashīd ad-Dīn must have been of Jewish origin.

A further argument with regard to Rashīd ad-Dīn's having once been a Jew can also be employed. We referred above to the Jew Rashīd *ad-Daula* at the Court of Gaykhātū. We do not think we are wrong in expressing the opinion that this Rashīd ad-Daula was no other than the Rashīd *ad-Dīn* of the days of Ghāzān. In the interval between his first appearance under Gaykhātū (1294) and his appointment as vizier (1299), Saul had become Paul, the Jew had turned Muslim, Rashīd ad-Daula had been transformed into Rashīd ad-Dīn.

This assumption of identity can hardly be disputed on account of the change of name. We find him, even in his capacity of Muslim Vizier, being frequently referred to as Rashīd ad-Daula in the sources. Mufaḍḍal b. abi'l Faḍā'il,[1] when he mentions رشيد الدولة الوزير المتطبب مشير دولة ملك التتار means him; and other historians, too, speak of him as رشيد الدولة.[2] This confusion of the sources implies a measure of uncertainty worthy of remark, for it would be definitely unthinkable in the case of an individual of indisputably Muslim origin. The variation and confusion between "Daula" and "Dīn" in our sources receives its explanation in the statement of such an authority as E. Blochet[3] that "les titres en al-Moulk et en ad-Daula . . . sont caractéristiques des fonctionnaires de l'administration qui ne sont point Musulmans, les sectateurs du Prophète recevant, comme cela est parfaitement logique, les mêmes titres en ad-Dīn . . ." But even without these considerations we possess unequivocal evidence regarding the Jewish origin of this Rashīd ad-Dīn in a statement, according to which

[1] *Mufaḍḍal b. abi'l Faḍā'il*, vol. xiv, pp. 660–1; vol. xx, p. 226.

[2] See E. Blochet, *Introduction*, p. 50: رشيد الدولة ابو الفضل . . . الطبيب اولا وزير قازان.

[3] Note in Blochet's edition of *Mufaḍḍal ibn abi'l Faḍā'il*, vol. xx, p. 36.

Rashīd ad-Dīn said of himself: "And I was a simple Jew, an apothecary, a physician, a poor man among my fellows . . .," [1] and in the still more reliable evidence of the Arab geographer Ibn Baṭūṭa who spent the year 1325 at Baghdād, where he met the Vizier of the Īl-Khān Abū Sa'īd, a certain Ghiyāth ad-Dīn Muḥammad b. Khodja Rashīd (ابن خواجة رشيد)—the son of our Rashīd ad-Dīn—who was, according to Ibn Baṭūṭa, "one of the Jewish emigrants".[2]

The statements of contemporaries also corroborate the account as to the manner of Rashīd ad-Dīn's death. One might say that his end expresses the fate of a Jew in the service of alien powers. Exactly as in the case of Sa'd ad-Daula,[3] his enemies, in order to be rid of Rashīd ad-Dīn, accused him of having poisoned the Īl-Khān Uljāytū, and executed him in 1318 at the age of over 70, together with his son Ibrāhīm. His head was sent to Tabrīz and dragged through the town, while proclamation was made: "This is the head of the Jew who has dishonoured the word of God, may God's curse be upon him." [4] So widespread was the belief that he was a Jew that even a century after his death the ruler of Tabrīz, Mīrānshāh, had his bones exhumed in the Muslim cemetery of Tabrīz in order to reinter them in the Jewish cemetery, so that he should not lie together with true Muslims.

The end of Rashīd ad-Dīn sealed the fate of Persian and 'Irāqian Jewry and marked the complete elimination of the Jews from public life for centuries. Yet, as so frequently happened in Jewish history, the destruction of political and economic influence led to a spiritual revival and to a period of internal growth. The birth of Hebrew-Persian literature [5]

[1] Cited by Blochet, *Introduction*, p. 30. [2] *Ibn Baṭūṭa*, ii, 116.

[3] A historic parallel which is really remarkable.

[4] Cf. Blochet, *Introduction*, pp. 30 and 51. Howorth, *History of the Mongols*, pp. 588–9.

[5] For a general account of Judæo-Persian literature see E. N. Adler, *The Persian Jews, their Books and Ritual*, London, 1899; W. Bacher, in *Jewish Encyclopedia*, vii, pp. 317–324; and now W. Fischel, in *Encycl. Jud.*, ix, col. 557–568, and in *MGWJ.*, 1933, pp. 113–127.

falls in that gloomy political period, in which Jewry symbolically experienced its political and economic fall in the person of Sa'd ad-Daula and Rashīd ad-Dīn, and it was at that very time that the first great Jewish-Persian poet, Maulāna Shāhīn of Shīrāz, "the Firdūsi of Persian Jewry," appeared on the scene.

D. APPENDIX

Arabic Sources for the History of the Baghdād Gaonate in the Thirteenth Century

WHEN Jews are mentioned by name in the works of Arab historians, the reason should be sought in their particular importance for the public life of their period. A number of those Jewish personalities, who played a leading and active part in the political or economic life of Islam, have been dealt with in the previous chapters. In the Arabic chronicles, and particularly in those of 'Irāq in the thirteenth century, we also meet the names of Jews who did their work within their own community, but who are mentioned there as having been the official representatives of their community. Usually these were the heads of the Jewish Academy in Baghdād, the " Ra's Mathība " or " Gaon ".[1] They are made the subject of this appendix because the material concerning them in the Arabic sources shows yet another angle of the relationship between the Islamic state of the Middle Ages and Babylonian Jewry.

While the institution of the Exilarch, the " Resh Galūta," (رأس الجالوت) did find certain references in Arabic literature,[2] the institution of the " Resh Methībta ", the Gaon, could scarcely be identified in Arabic sources. We learn, however, now from the Arabic chronicle of *Ibn as-Sā'i*,[3] only recently published, and from that of *Ibn al-Fuwaṭi*,[4] that the Gaonate is also dealt with by the

[1] In the thirteenth century Baghdād Jewry was represented by the heads of the Academy. The latter regarded themselves as the legitimate successors of the Gaonim of Sura and Pumbadita and also styled themselves Gaon or Ra's Methībta.

[2] J. Goldziher, " Renseignements de source musulmane sur la dignité de Resch Galuta " (*REJ.*, 1884, vol. viii, pp. 121 ff.).

[3] al-Jāmi' al-Mukhtaṣar, Baghdād, 1934. On him see F. Wüstenfeld, *Die Geschichtschreiber der Araber*, Göttingen, 1881–2, No. 354. A short history by this author has appeared under the title *Mukhtaṣar akhbār al-Khulafā*, Būlāq, 1309/1891. This, however, is not the work meant here.

[4] al-Ḥawādith al-Jāmi'a, Baghdād, 1932. *Vide* F. Wüstenfeld, op. cit., No. 387, and the introduction to this *Chronicle* by the editor.

Arab historians; and thanks to their works we now have fresh data regarding a number of Gaonim and other prominent Baghdād Jews of the period. Thus we learn of the following Baghdād Gaonim, who possessed the title " Ra's Mathībat alyahūd " (رأس مثيبة اليهود)[1]:—

1. Dāniyāl b. al-'Āzar b. Hibatallah
2. Hibatallah b. Abi'r-Rabī'
3. Abu'l Fatḥ Isḥāq b. ash-Shuwaikh
4. Dāniyāl b. Shamū'īl b. Abi'r-Rabī'
5. 'Ēli b. Zakhariyyā

Also of the following outstanding Baghdād Jews:—

6. Abū Ṭāhir b. Shibr and his son Abū Ghālib
7. Ibn Karam
8. 'Izz ad-Daula b. Kammūna.

The information to be found in the Arabic sources regarding these persons is all the more important for Jewish historical study because Hebrew sources for this period are exceptionally scanty. Almost all our information goes back to the Hebrew Dīwān of El'āzār b. Ya'qōb Hababli,[2] which was first used by S. Poznanski in his work on the Babylonian Gaonim and for the earlier period to the Iggroth of Rabbi Samuel b. 'Ali. It is only natural that with such paucity of Hebrew material a number of problems regarding this scarcely investigated century of Jewish history have had to remain unanswered. Even though the new Arabic material does not answer all questions, it permits us to fill up numerous gaps in our knowledge in many points clarifying

[1] This expression occurs in *Ibn as-Sā'i* on pp. 266–9, 283; in *Ibn al-Fuwaṭi* on pp. 13, 218, 224, 248. The editors of these chronicles suggested various emendations of that expression, the meaning of which was not clear to them.

[2] This Dīwān was brought from Aleppo to Europe in 1898 by Elkan Nathan Adler. The author lived between 1195 and 1250 in Baghdād, where he seems to have been the domestic poet of leading Jewish circles. Since he makes the concrete causes of the composition of his poems clear in both the superscriptions and the texts of his verses, mentioning the names of the people concerning or for whom he wrote by name and titles, his Dīwān, quite apart from its poetic value, is a true historic storehouse. Jewish scholars like Brody, Davidson, Poznanski, and Mann, have published sections of this Dīwān. The entire Dīwān has just been issued by H. Brody, Jerusalem, 1936.

several uncertainties regarding the development of the Babylonian Gaonate.

The following are the Arabic passages referring to the personalities of Baghdād Jewry mentioned above. They are literally translated and a minimum of explanation added. We trust that they will serve as raw material for further investigations by students of Jewish history.

1. *Dāniyāl b. al-'Āzar b. Hibatallah* دانيال بن العازر بن هبة الله

" On the ninth of Dhu'l Qa'da (605/1209) the Caliph appointed Ibn Hibat (allah) as head of the Academy of the Jews (رأس مثيبة اليهود), and issued a document regarding this. He handed it over to him, and the latter read it to the Jews in their synagogue. And this is its text."

(The first half of the text consists of general formulas which can be omitted here. The second deals directly with Dāniyāl's appointment to office, and reads :—)

" Since Dāniyāl b. al-'Āzar b. Hibatallah hath petitioned us to appoint him as Head of the School (Ra's mathība), in place of the deceased al-'Āzar b. Hilāl b. Fahd, according to the same rules and customs, and since it hath been learnt in what manner he is famed among his coreligionists and what (good) qualities are attributed to him, and that he doth show himself worthy of (the granting of) his petition by his good manner of life among them and spotlessness of character, His Majesty an Nāṣir li-dīn Allahi . . . hath ordained that he (i.e. the petitioner) shall be appointed Ra's Mathība after the fashion of the above-mentioned deceased, in so far as Ibn ad-Dastūr was likewise Ra's Mathība. Let him be regarded in this capacity by all places which are customarily subject to his administration and disposal. He may distinguish himself from his fellows by the garb permitted to people of his rank. It is the duty of the Jewish community and its judges in Baghdād and the districts of 'Irāq to submit to that which he orders, to demean themselves according to his word in the disposition of their affairs, and to act according to the degree required thereby (i.e. by his order). They must allow him all those rights customarily claimed by his predecessors in this

Dignity, in all places over which his administration extends without opposing any resistance to him therein ; while he himself shall act in accordance with the provisions of Protection (afforded to the ahl adh-Dhimma) in all that he does or orders, and inviolably and faithfully fulfils the observances (the Orders of the Government) and the requirements of Refuge (i.e. refuge in the goal of all protection, namely the Caliph) and of reverence, according to the Will of God upon which we build. Written this the 9. Dhu'l-Qa'da of the year 605. Praised be God alone and His blessings on our Lord the prophet Muḥammed, etc."

Ibn as-Sā'i, pp. 266–9.

Cf. Poznanski, op. cit., pp. 10–11, 37–9.

Iggroth R. Samuel b. Ali, p. 30, and J. Mann, *Texts and Studies*, pp. 222 ff. The engrossing of a document (عهدة) seems to have been an essential element of the appointment. See *Shebet Yehūda*, ed. Wiener No. 42 ; *Benjamin of Tudela*, ed. Asher, i, 62. About the text of appointment of a Nagīd, cf. Qalqashandi, *Ṣubḥ*, xi, pp. 385 ff. See Gottheil, *JQR.*, xix, o.s., pp. 429–501.

The chief of the Christian Community in Babylonia, the Catholicus, was also appointed to his office by the Caliph and a corresponding document issued. Such a document has been preserved ; cf. H. F. Amedroz, " The Tadhkira of Ibn Ḥamdūn," *JRAS.*, 1908, pp. 447–450, 467–470. See also A. v. Kremer, *ZDMG.*, viii, p. 219.

2. *Hibatallah b. Abi'r-Rabī'* (هبة الله بن ابي الربيع)

" Hibatallah b. Abi'r-Rabī', the Dhimmi—head of the Academy of the Jews—was learned in medicine and philosophy, wrote an excellent hand and died in Dhu'l Ḥijja 606/1210 at the age of over 60 years."

Ibn as-Sā'i, p. 283. We know nothing as yet from Hebrew sources regarding this Gaon Nathaniel (= Hibatallah) of Baghdād.

3. *Abu'l Fatḥ Isḥāq b. ash-Shuwaikh*
(ابو الفتح اسحاق بن الشويخ)

" In this year (645/1247–8) died Abu'l Fatḥ Isḥāq b. ash-Shuwaikh, head of the Academy of the Jews. He was a charitable and cultured man, wrote a beautiful hand, composed excellent poems, and had a magnificent knowledge of astronomy."

Ibn al-Fuwaṭi, p. 224. He is relatively one of the best known Gaonim of the thirteenth century. See *Poznanski*, pp. 42–6, where all the Hebrew material concerning him is collected. There was no definite information, however, regarding the length of his term of office. Al-Ḥarīzi found him already in office in 1221.

The knowledge of this Gaon's year of death (645/1247) does at last provide a fixed point in his own chronology as well as in that of the Baghdād Gaonate in general.

We also learn of an interesting incident which occurred during his term of office.

"At the beginning of Muḥarram (of the year 627/1228), Muḥyi ad-Dīn Abū 'Abdallah Muḥammad b. Faḍlān sat in the Dīwān of the Head Tax and demanded the head tax (جزية) from the ahl adh-Dhimma. One of these stood before him and waited till his head tax had been weighed and a receipt given to him. This was humiliating and they suffered greatly therefrom. There was an Abū 'Alī b. al-Masīḥi, the chief of the physicians. He enjoyed privileges and free access to the house of the Caliph. He claimed that he was sick, excused himself (to the Dīwān), and therefore applied to have his head tax paid by his son. That was not permitted, and he appeared and paid it.

Once there came Ibn ash-Shuwaikh, the head of the Academy of the Jews, to his house (i.e. that of the chief of the Dīwān) *at night*, and requested him to receive his head tax from him then. But the other would not accede, explaining, 'It is unavoidable for you to come to the Dīwān *by day* and pay the head tax.' He was very strict regarding this and would not satisfy any wish."

Ibn al-Fuwaṭi, p. 13. This anecdote relates how a Christian notable and the Gaon, the head of the Jewish Academy, were rebuffed with scant respect when they attempted to avoid complying with the humiliating procedure accompanying the payment of the head tax. It throws light on the political and social standing of the representatives of the "ahl adh-Dhimma", including the Gaon, at that period. See aṣ-Ṣūli, *Adab al-Kuttāb*, pp. 213–16, and *Führer durch die Ausstellung Papyrus Rainer*, Wien, 1894, p. 177.

4. *Dāniyāl b. Shamū'īl b. Abi'r-Rabī'*

(دانيال بن شمويل بن ابى الربيع)

"In this year (645/1247) Dāniyāl b. Shamū'īl b. Abi'r-Rabī' was appointed chief of the Academy. The Vizier Mu'ayyad ad-Dīn Muḥammad b. al-'Alqami brought him before the chief Judge 'Abd ar-Raḥmān b. al-Lamghāni, let him take a place before him, and spoke to him: 'I have appointed thee leader of the folk of thy community, over the folk of thy faith which hath been abolished by the Mohammedan law, that thou mayst lead them within the boundaries of their religion. Thou shalt order them regarding those things commanded by their religion and those things forbidden by their religion. Thou shalt decide between them in their conflicts and legal disputes according to their religion, and the praise of God be over Islam.'

"Then he (the Jewish Chief) arose, donned his cloak in the ante-room of the Judge, and went home on foot, together with a group of Jews and a group of the followers of the Dīwān. A group of the people set themselves in his way in order to stone him; but they were not permitted to do this, and were prevented. Part of them were caught, arrested, imprisoned, and punished."

Ibn al-Fuwaṭi, p. 218. According to the Dīwān of El'āzār Hababli, the successor of Ibn ash-Shuwaikh was a certain Dāniyāl b. Abi'r-Rabī'; but he provided no further details; even his term of office could only be guessed at. *Poznanski*, p. 47, set it between 1240 and 1250. But thanks to the precise date of the death of his predecessor, Ibn ash-Shuwaikh, the year of his entry into office must be fixed at 1247–8. Ibn al-Fuwaṭi, in fact, informs us that Dāniyāl was appointed Gaon in the year of his predecessor's death. It is now also possible to fix the length of his term of office, since we learn from Ibn al-Fuwaṭi that a new Gaon entered into office in 1250.

The attempt to stone the newly appointed Gaon illustrates the loss of the prestige possessed in former centuries by the representatives of Babylonian Jewry.

5. *'Ēli b. Zakhariyyā of Arbil* (عالى بن زخريا الاربلى)

"In this year (648/1250), 'Ēli b. Zakhariyyā, the Jew of Arbil, applied to be appointed chief of the Jewish Academy.

This was granted. The Vizier discussed the situation with him and referred him to the Chief Judge. The latter permitted him to appear before him, and after praising Allah and his prophet he said to him: 'Therefore I have appointed thee leader of the folk of thy religion—a religion abolished by the Law of Islam, which may Allah permit to continue so long as Heaven and Earth exist—upon the condition that thou judge between those who bring their disputes before thee; thou shalt order them in accordance with that which is commanded in their religion and thou shalt forbid them in accordance with that which is forbidden in their religion.' Then he arose from before him, donned his cloak in the ante-room of the Judge, and with him through the Bāb an-Nūbi went a group of Jews and followers. He took with him the Decree of Appointment which had been written for him in the Dīwān."

Ibn al-Fuwaṭi, p. 248.

This text corresponds in its essential points to that of the former Gaon's induction into office.

'Ēli b. Zakhariyyā, whose full name has now been transmitted to us by the Arabic historian, is undoubtedly identical with the Gaon 'Ali, whom Poznanski designates 'Ali II. This identification is supported by the few details which we know concerning this Gaon. About 'Ali (علي) and 'Ēli (عالي) cf. Steinschneider, *JQR.*, xi, p. 484, and Poznanski, *REJ.*, xxxiii, p. 319. About the Jewish community in Arbil at that time, cf. S. Assaf, *Iggroth of R. Samuel b. 'Ali*, p. 20.

Thanks to the Arabic sources, we now possess data which permit us to gauge the term of office of his predecessor, Dāniyāl b. Abi'r-Rabī', who became Gaon in 645/1247, and was therefore in office for only three years. This short period is very surprising. Whereas the document quoted above states, "In this year Dāniyāl b. Abi'r-Rabī' was appointed Gaon," it is stated here that "'Ēli b. Zakhariyyā, the Jew of Arbil, applied to be appointed". Did internal disputes bring the Gaonate of Dāniyāl to an early end, and could claimants to the Gaonate appear who were in a position to demand nomination to the position of Gaon from the Government authorities? New sources may possibly permit us to answer these questions.

After this 'Ēli b. Zakhariyyā, Ibn al-Fuwaṭi tells us nothing about fresh nominations of Gaonim, although he continues his account of events in Baghdād and 'Irāq after 648/1250 down to 700/1301, with continual references to Jews and Jewish affairs. Should it be assumed that 'Ēli b. Zakhariyyā was the last Gaon? That, however, would contradict the fact that Hebrew sources tell us of a Gaon named Samuel b. Daniel in Baghdād in the year 1288.

'Ēli b. Zakhariyyā's term of office coincides with one of the liveliest epochs in the history of Babylonian Jewry. The irruption of the Mongols, the fall of Baghdād, and the collapse of the 'Abbāsid Caliphs occurred during his office. In the changes wrought by the new domination of the Mongols, one of the results was that the concept of the ahl adh-Dhimma lost its meaning. The appointment of a Gaon may have become a purely internal affair of the Jewish community. That naturally would no longer interest the Arabic chronicler, who had apparently registered the nomination of Gaonim because this was an administrative act illuminating the relationship between the "protected people" and Islam.

Together with the information regarding the Gaonim, the two Arabic chroniclers furnish us with some details of other outstanding personalities in Baghdād Jewry during the thirteenth century.

6. *Abū Ṭāhir b. Shibr* (ابو طاهر بن شبر)

"Abu Ṭāhir b. Shibr, Jahbadh (جهبذ) of the Dīwān al-'Azīz, was chief of the Jews (رئيس اليهود), and died at the end of the month of Ramaḍān in the year 601/1204–5. He was brought to Mount aṭ-Ṭūr (the Mount of Olives at Jerusalem) and buried there."

Ibn as-Sā'i, pp. 162–3.

"In the same year died also Abū Ghālib b. Abi Ṭāhir b. Shibr, the Jew, an official of the Mint (دار الضرب)."

Ibn as-Sā'i, p. 166.

This is the first intimation of the presence of these Jewish officials in the financial administration of Baghdād at that time. The death of both father and son in the same year is somewhat remarkable. Cf. al-Ḥarīzi, chap. 46.

7. *Ibn Karam* (ابن كرم)

" When Abu'ṭ-Ṭulaiq . . . met one of the leaders of the Christians or the Jews riding, he made him descend and insulted him. He did so with the physician Ibn Tūmā' and later with his son, and also with Ibn Karam, the Jew."

Ibn al-Fuwaṭi, p. 150, under the year 639/1241.

The Dīwān of El'āzār Hababli contains certain poems written in honour of the Karam family which have been published by H. Brody in Ha-Zofeh (Budapest, vi, pp. 123–133). These poems obviously deal with a respected and influential family in Baghdād Jewry, of which we hitherto knew no more than the names of a few members. Our Arab chronicler now extends our knowledge regarding this family in an interesting fashion. What we should actually understand from the phrase " one of the leaders of the Jews " (احد من روساء اليهود) is hard to say. El'āzār Hababli also calls him only ראים. It is possible that as one of the notables of Baghdād Jewry he had won himself a special place in the economic life which had afforded him the privilege of riding through the streets of Baghdād—a privilege denied the ahl adh-Dhimma in general.

8. *'Izz ad-Daula b. Kammūna* (عزّ الدولة بن كمّونة)

" In this year (683/1284) it became known in Baghdād that 'Izz ad-Daula b. Kammūna the Jew had written a book entitled ' Investigations regarding the Three Religions . . .' The people rose up in excitement and gathered together in order to penetrate into his house and slay him. Thereupon . . . the prefect of 'Irāq, Majd ad-Dīn b. al-Athīr and a group of officials rose to the Mustanṣiriyya and summoned the Supreme Judge and the teachers to him in order to clarify this situation. They sought for Ibn Kammūna, but he kept himself hidden. When the Supreme Judge rode to prayer on this day, which happened to be a Friday, it happened that the crowds prevented him doing so, and he turned back to the Mustanṣiriyya. Ibn al-Athīr went forth to calm the crowds, but these showered abuse upon him and accused him of belonging to the part of Ibn Kammūna and protecting him. Thereupon the Governor ordered, through an official proclamation, that they should assemble outside the walls of Baghdād the following morning in order to witness the burning of Ibn Kammūna. Thereupon the people calmed themselves and no longer referred to him.

Regarding Ibn Kammūna, he was placed in a leather-covered box and carried to Ḥilla, where his son was secretary; there he spent his days and also died."

Ibn al-Fuwaṭi, pp. 441–2.

M. Steinschneider (*Die Arabische Literatur der Juden*, p. 240) has emphasized the value of Ibn Kammūna's theological works. L. Hirschfeld (*Sa'd b. Mansur b. Kammunah*, Berlin, 1893) published a part of Ibn Kammūna's polemical works in his monograph, and D. H. Baneth (Ibn Kammūna, *MGWJ.*, 1925, vol. 69, pp. 295–311) has newly treated all matters relating to the work of this philosopher. But hitherto nothing definite was known regarding his life and personal lot. Neither the period nor locality of his activities was certain, while even the question whether he remained a Jew or was converted to Islam was a subject of controversy. L. Hirschfeld's lament (loc. cit., p. 7) that "scarcely the most meagre details regarding this author and the events of his life have come down to us" was hitherto justified. Now, however, Ibn al-Fuwaṭi steps into the breach and enriches our store of knowledge.

This highly notable report permits us to begin to clarify a number of questions associated with the life of this Jewish philosopher :—

(*a*) First regarding his alleged conversion to Islam. D. H. Baneth has already proved clearly that from Ibn Kammūna's theological attitude to Islam as manifested in his works, and his express statements against every kind of renegade, it is now evident that he never became a Muslim. The above quotation confirms this in every respect. To begin with, an historian like Ibn al-Fuwaṭi used to record conversions to Islam, and would assuredly have done so had such a thing occurred to a person of the standing of Ibn Kammūna, who bore the title "'Izz ad-Daula" and had a name in the world of Islam at that period. Secondly, it is almost impossible that the people would take up against a Muslim the attitude which is reported here. Nothing more seems to be shown by the opposition to Ibn Kammūna than the dislike of a possibly incited crowd for a Jew who dared to express heretical views regarding Islam and its prophet.

(*b*) With regard to the period of his activity, the only references were to be found at the end of individual manuscripts which differed considerably from one another. The statement " he became known in the year 1284/683 " now gives a definite and reliable date. It can be assumed that he did not live too long in his exile and probably died in the same year.

(*c*) Ibn al-Fuwaṭi also clears up the place of his activity; M. Steinschneider (*Die Arab. Literatur*, p. 239) had considered Egypt to be Ibn Kammūna's place of residence. Baneth (loc. cit., p. 308), however, largely on chronological grounds, had suggested " the region under the rule of the Mongol Īl-Khāns " as the geographical sphere of Ibn Kammūna. We now know that he did actually live in Baghdād at the period of the Īl-Khān Abāqā, spending the evening of his life at Ḥilla in the vicinity of Baghdād. Also his family had been living in 'Irāq for some time, as we learn from a passage in *Ibn as-Sā'i*, p. 163, that Abū Ghālib b. Kammūna the Jew died in the vault of Wāsiṭ in the year 601/1204–5. This was probably his grandfather or another member of this well-known family.

INDEX

Rashīd ad-Dīn, 122–5
Rūzbah, Jewish Governor of Sirāf, 32

S

Saadya Gaon al-Fayyūmi, 35, 44
Sa'd ad-Daula b. Ṣafī ad-Daula al-yahūdi, Chapter C *passim*
Ṣadr ad-Dīn Aḥmad ar-Razzāq, 118
Sahl b. Naẓīr, 5, 32, 42
Sahl b. Neṭīra, 37, 40, 42 sq.
Samau' al b. 'Ādiyā al-yahūdi, 46
Samuel b. 'Ali, 127, 132
Samuel b. Daniel hakohen, 107, 133
Shāhīn of Shīrāz, 125
Shams ad-Daula b. Majd ad-Daula, 104, 111
Sulaymān b. 'Ushara, 55

T

Tāj ad-Dīn b. Mukhāṭir, 104
Tughān, Emīr, 112, 114
Tughārjār, Emīr, 114, 118

U

'Ubaidallah b. Yaḥyā al-Khāqāni, 11, 12, 28
'Ubaidallah b. Sulaymān, 6
Uljāytū Khān, 95, 121, 122, 124

Y

Ya'qūb, a money changer, 32
Ya'qūb b. Killis, Chapter B I *passim*
Yārūkh *vide* Bārūkh
al-Yāzūri, Abū Muḥammad Ḥasan 81, 85

Z

aẓ-Ẓāhir, 32, 68, 71 sq., 74 sq., 79
Zain ad-Dīn 'Ali b. Sa'īd, 114
Zakariyyā b. Yūḥanna, 5, 9